JAPANESE

V O C A B U L A R Y

FOR ENGLISH SPEAKERS

ENGLISH-JAPANESE

The most useful words
To expand your lexicon and sharpen
your language skills

5000 words

Japanese vocabulary for English speakers - 5000 words

By Andrey Taranov

T&P Books vocabularies are intended for helping you learn, memorize and review foreign words. The dictionary is divided into themes, covering all major spheres of everyday activities, business, science, culture, etc.

The process of learning words using T&P Books' theme-based dictionaries gives you the following advantages:

- Correctly grouped source information predetermines success at subsequent stages of word memorization
- Availability of words derived from the same root allowing memorization of word units (rather than separate words)
- Small units of words facilitate the process of establishing associative links needed for consolidation of vocabulary
- Level of language knowledge can be estimated by the number of learned words

T&P Books Publishing
www.tpbooks.com

ISBN: 978-1-78314-245-3

This book is also available in E-book formats.
Please visit www.tpbooks.com or the major online bookstores.

JAPANESE VOCABULARY
for English speakers

T&P Books vocabularies are intended to help you learn, memorize, and review foreign words. The vocabulary contains over 5000 commonly used words arranged thematically.

- Vocabulary contains the most commonly used words
- Recommended as an addition to any language course
- Meets the needs of beginners and advanced learners of foreign languages
- Convenient for daily use, revision sessions, and self-testing activities
- Allows you to assess your vocabulary

Special features of the vocabulary

- Words are organized according to their meaning, not alphabetically
- Words are presented in three columns to facilitate the reviewing and self-testing processes
- Words in groups are divided into small blocks to facilitate the learning process
- The vocabulary offers a convenient and simple transcription of each foreign word

The vocabulary has 155 topics including:

Basic Concepts, Numbers, Colors, Months, Seasons, Units of Measurement, Clothing & Accessories, Food & Nutrition, Restaurant, Family Members, Relatives, Character, Feelings, Emotions, Diseases, City, Town, Sightseeing, Shopping, Money, House, Home, Office, Working in the Office, Import & Export, Marketing, Job Search, Sports, Education, Computer, Internet, Tools, Nature, Countries, Nationalities and more ...

T&P BOOKS' THEME-BASED DICTIONARIES

The Correct System for Memorizing Foreign Words

Acquiring vocabulary is one of the most important elements of learning a foreign language, because words allow us to express our thoughts, ask questions, and provide answers. An inadequate vocabulary can impede communication with a foreigner and make it difficult to understand a book or movie well.

The pace of activity in all spheres of modern life, including the learning of modern languages, has increased. Today, we need to memorize large amounts of information (grammar rules, foreign words, etc.) within a short period. However, this does not need to be difficult. All you need to do is to choose the right training materials, learn a few special techniques, and develop your individual training system.

Having a system is critical to the process of language learning. Many people fail to succeed in this regard; they cannot master a foreign language because they fail to follow a system comprised of selecting materials, organizing lessons, arranging new words to be learned, and so on. The lack of a system causes confusion and eventually, lowers self-confidence.

T&P Books' theme-based dictionaries can be included in the list of elements needed for creating an effective system for learning foreign words. These dictionaries were specially developed for learning purposes and are meant to help students effectively memorize words and expand their vocabulary.

Generally speaking, the process of learning words consists of three main elements:

- Reception (creation or acquisition) of a training material, such as a word list
- Work aimed at memorizing new words
- Work aimed at reviewing the learned words, such as self-testing

All three elements are equally important since they determine the quality of work and the final result. All three processes require certain skills and a well-thought-out approach.

New words are often encountered quite randomly when learning a foreign language and it may be difficult to include them all in a unified list. As a result, these words remain written on scraps of paper, in book margins, textbooks, and so on. In order to systematize such words, we have to create and continually update a "book of new words." A paper notebook, a netbook, or a tablet PC can be used for these purposes.

This "book of new words" will be your personal, unique list of words. However, it will only contain the words that you came across during the learning process. For example, you might have written down the words "Sunday," "Tuesday," and "Friday." However, there are additional words for days of the week, for example, "Saturday," that are missing, and your list of words would be incomplete. Using a theme dictionary, in addition to the "book of new words," is a reasonable solution to this problem.

The theme-based dictionary may serve as the basis for expanding your vocabulary.

It will be your big "book of new words" containing the most frequently used words of a foreign language already included. There are quite a few theme-based dictionaries available, and you should ensure that you make the right choice in order to get the maximum benefit from your purchase.

Therefore, we suggest using theme-based dictionaries from T&P Books Publishing as an aid to learning foreign words. Our books are specially developed for effective use in the sphere of vocabulary systematization, expansion and review.

Theme-based dictionaries are not a magical solution to learning new words. However, they can serve as your main database to aid foreign-language acquisition. Apart from theme dictionaries, you can have copybooks for writing down new words, flash cards, glossaries for various texts, as well as other resources; however, a good theme dictionary will always remain your primary collection of words.

T&P Books' theme-based dictionaries are specialty books that contain the most frequently used words in a language.

The main characteristic of such dictionaries is the division of words into themes. For example, the *City* theme contains the words "street," "crossroads," "square," "fountain," and so on. The *Talking* theme might contain words like "to talk," "to ask," "question," and "answer".

All the words in a theme are divided into smaller units, each comprising 3–5 words. Such an arrangement improves the perception of words and makes the learning process less tiresome. Each unit contains a selection of words with similar meanings or identical roots. This allows you to learn words in small groups and establish other associative links that have a positive effect on memorization.

The words on each page are placed in three columns: a word in your native language, its translation, and its transcription. Such positioning allows for the use of techniques for effective memorization. After closing the translation column, you can flip through and review foreign words, and vice versa. "This is an easy and convenient method of review – one that we recommend you do often."

Our theme-based dictionaries contain transcriptions for all the foreign words. Unfortunately, none of the existing transcriptions are able to convey the exact nuances of foreign pronunciation. That is why we recommend using the transcriptions only as a supplementary learning aid. Correct pronunciation can only be acquired with the help of sound. Therefore our collection includes audio theme-based dictionaries.

The process of learning words using T&P Books' theme-based dictionaries gives you the following advantages:

- You have correctly grouped source information, which predetermines your success at subsequent stages of word memorization
- Availability of words derived from the same root (lazy, lazily, lazybones), allowing you to memorize word units instead of separate words
- Small units of words facilitate the process of establishing associative links needed for consolidation of vocabulary
- You can estimate the number of learned words and hence your level of language knowledge
- The dictionary allows for the creation of an effective and high-quality revision process
- You can revise certain themes several times, modifying the revision methods and techniques
- Audio versions of the dictionaries help you to work out the pronunciation of words and develop your skills of auditory word perception

The T&P Books' theme-based dictionaries are offered in several variants differing in the number of words: 1.500, 3.000, 5.000, 7.000, and 9.000 words. There are also dictionaries containing 15,000 words for some language combinations. Your choice of dictionary will depend on your knowledge level and goals.

We sincerely believe that our dictionaries will become your trusty assistant in learning foreign languages and will allow you to easily acquire the necessary vocabulary.

TABLE OF CONTENTS

T&P Books' Theme-Based Dictionaries   4
Pronunciation guide   13
Abbreviations   14

BASIC CONCEPTS   15
Basic concepts. Part 1   15

1. Pronouns   15
2. Greetings. Salutations. Farewells   15
3. How to address   16
4. Cardinal numbers. Part 1   16
5. Cardinal numbers. Part 2   18
6. Ordinal numbers   18
7. Numbers. Fractions   18
8. Numbers. Basic operations   19
9. Numbers. Miscellaneous   19
10. The most important verbs. Part 1   19
11. The most important verbs. Part 2   20
12. The most important verbs. Part 3   21
13. The most important verbs. Part 4   22
14. Colors   23
15. Questions   24
16. Prepositions   25
17. Function words. Adverbs. Part 1   25
18. Function words. Adverbs. Part 2   27

Basic concepts. Part 2   29

19. Weekdays   29
20. Hours. Day and night   29
21. Months. Seasons   30
22. Units of measurement   32
23. Containers   33

HUMAN BEING   35
Human being. The body   35

24. Head   35
25. Human body   36

Clothing & Accessories 38

26. Outerwear. Coats 38
27. Men's & women's clothing 38
28. Clothing. Underwear 39
29. Headwear 39
30. Footwear 39
31. Personal accessories 40
32. Clothing. Miscellaneous 40
33. Personal care. Cosmetics 41
34. Watches. Clocks 42

Food. Nutricion 44

35. Food 44
36. Drinks 45
37. Vegetables 47
38. Fruits. Nuts 47
39. Bread. Candy 48
40. Cooked dishes 49
41. Spices 50
42. Meals 50
43. Table setting 51
44. Restaurant 51

Family, relatives and friends 53

45. Personal information. Forms 53
46. Family members. Relatives 53

Medicine 55

47. Diseases 55
48. Symptoms. Treatments. Part 1 56
49. Symptoms. Treatments. Part 2 57
50. Symptoms. Treatments. Part 3 58
51. Doctors 59
52. Medicine. Drugs. Accessories 59

HUMAN HABITAT 61
City 61

53. City. Life in the city 61
54. Urban institutions 62
55. Signs 64
56. Urban transportation 65

57. Sightseeing   66
58. Shopping   66
59. Money   67
60. Post. Postal service   68

Dwelling. House. Home   70

61. House. Electricity   70
62. Villa. Mansion   70
63. Apartment   71
64. Furniture. Interior   71
65. Bedding   72
66. Kitchen   72
67. Bathroom   73
68. Household appliances   74

HUMAN ACTIVITIES   76
Job. Business. Part 1   76

69. Office. Working in the office   76
70. Business processes. Part 1   77
71. Business processes. Part 2   78
72. Production. Works   79
73. Contract. Agreement   81
74. Import & Export   81
75. Finances   82
76. Marketing   83
77. Advertising   83
78. Banking   84
79. Telephone. Phone conversation   85
80. Mobile telephone   85
81. Stationery   86
82. Kinds of business   86

Job. Business. Part 2   89

83. Show. Exhibition   89
84. Science. Research. Scientists   90

Professions and occupations   92

85. Job search. Dismissal   92
86. Business people   92
87. Service professions   94
88. Military professions and ranks   94
89. Officials. Priests   95

90. Agricultural professions   96
91. Art professions   96
92. Various professions   97
93. Occupations. Social status   98

Education   100

94. School   100
95. College. University   101
96. Sciences. Disciplines   102
97. Writing system. Orthography   102
98. Foreign languages   104

Rest. Entertainment. Travel   106

99. Trip. Travel   106
100. Hotel   107

TECHNICAL EQUIPMENT. TRANSPORTATION 108
Technical equipment   108

101. Computer   108
102. Internet. E-mail   109
103. Electricity   110
104. Tools   111

Transportation   114

105. Airplane   114
106. Train   115
107. Ship   116
108. Airport   117

Life events   119

109. Holidays. Event   119
110. Funerals. Burial   120
111. War. Soldiers   121
112. War. Military actions. Part 1   122
113. War. Military actions. Part 2   123
114. Weapons   125
115. Ancient people   126
116. Middle Ages   127
117. Leader. Chief. Authorities   129
118. Breaking the law. Criminals. Part 1 129
119. Breaking the law. Criminals. Part 2 131

120. Police. Law. Part 1   132
121. Police. Law. Part 2   133

NATURE   135
The Earth. Part 1   135

122. Outer space   135
123. The Earth   136
124. Cardinal directions   137
125. Sea. Ocean   137
126. Seas' and Oceans' names   138
127. Mountains   139
128. Mountains names   140
129. Rivers   140
130. Rivers' names   141
131. Forest   142
132. Natural resources   143

The Earth. Part 2   145

133. Weather   145
134. Severe weather. Natural disasters   146

Fauna   147

135. Mammals. Predators   147
136. Wild animals   147
137. Domestic animals   149
138. Birds   150
139. Fish. Marine animals   151
140. Amphibians. Reptiles   152
141. Insects   152

Flora   154

142. Trees   154
143. Shrubs   155
144. Fruits. Berries   155
145. Flowers. Plants   156
146. Cereals, grains   157

COUNTRIES. NATIONALITIES   158

147. Western Europe   158
148. Central and Eastern Europe   158
149. Former USSR countries   159

150. Asia   159
151. North America   160
152. Central and South America   160
153. Africa   161
154. Australia. Oceania   161
155. Cities   161

PRONUNCIATION GUIDE

Hiragana	Katakana	Rōmaji	Japanese example	T&P phonetic alphabet	English example

Consonants

Hiragana	Katakana	Rōmaji	Japanese example	T&P phonetic alphabet	English example
あ	ア	a	あなた	[a]	shorter than in ask
い	イ	i	いす	[i], [i:]	feet, Peter
う	ウ	u	うた	[u], [u:]	book, shoe
え	エ	e	いいえ	[e]	elm, medal
お	オ	o	しお	[ɔ]	bottle, doctor
や	ヤ	ya	やすみ	[jɑ]	young, yard
ゆ	ユ	yu	ふゆ	[ju]	youth, usually
よ	ヨ	yo	ようす	[jɔ]	New York

Syllables

Hiragana	Katakana	Rōmaji	Japanese example	T&P phonetic alphabet	English example
ば	バ	b	ばん	[b]	baby, book
ち	チ	ch	ちち	[tʃ]	cheese
だ	ダ	d	からだ	[d]	day, doctor
ふ	フ	f	ひふ	[f]	face, food
が	ガ	g	がっこう	[g]	game, gold
は	ハ	h	はは	[h]	home, have
じ	ジ	j	じしょ	[dʒ]	joke, general
か	カ	k	かぎ	[k]	clock, kiss
む	ム	m	さむらい	[m]	magic, milk
に	ニ	n	にもつ	[n]	name, normal
ぱ	パ	p	パン	[p]	pencil, private
ら	ラ	r	いくら	[r]	rice, radio
さ	サ	s	あさ	[s]	city, boss
し	シ	sh	わたし	[ɕ]	sheep, shop
た	タ	t	ふた	[t]	tourist, trip
つ	ツ	ts	いくつ	[ts]	cats, tsetse fly
わ	ワ	w	わた	[w]	vase, winter
ざ	ザ	z	ざっし	[dz]	beads, kids

ABBREVIATIONS
used in the vocabulary

ab.	-	about
adj	-	adjective
adv	-	adverb
anim.	-	animate
as adj	-	attributive noun used as adjective
e.g.	-	for example
etc.	-	et cetera
fam.	-	familiar
fem.	-	feminine
form.	-	formal
inanim.	-	inanimate
masc.	-	masculine
math	-	mathematics
mil.	-	military
n	-	noun
pl	-	plural
pron.	-	pronoun
sb	-	somebody
sing.	-	singular
sth	-	something
v aux	-	auxiliary verb
vi	-	intransitive verb
vi, vt	-	intransitive, transitive verb
vt	-	transitive verb

BASIC CONCEPTS

Basic concepts. Part 1

1. Pronouns

I, me	私	watashi
you	あなた	anata
he	彼	kare
she	彼女	kanojo
we	私たち	watashi tachi
you (to a group)	あなたがた	anata ga ta
they	彼らは	karera wa

2. Greetings. Salutations. Farewells

Hello! (fam.)	やあ！	yā!
Hello! (form.)	こんにちは！	konnichiwa!
Good morning!	おはよう！	ohayō!
Good afternoon!	こんにちは！	konnichiwa!
Good evening!	こんばんは！	konbanwa!
to say hello	こんにちはと言う	konnichiwa to iu
Hi! (hello)	やあ！	yā!
greeting (n)	挨拶	aisatsu
to greet (vt)	挨拶する	aisatsu suru
How are you?	元気？	genki ?
How are you? (form.)	お元気ですか？	wo genki desu ka?
How are you? (fam.)	元気？	genki ?
What's new?	調子はどう？	chōshi ha dō ?
Bye-Bye! Goodbye!	さようなら！	sayōnara!
Goodbye! (form.)	さようなら！	sayōnara!
Bye! (fam.)	バイバイ！	baibai!
See you soon!	じゃあね！	jā ne!
Farewell!	さらば！	saraba !
to say goodbye	別れを告げる	wakare wo tsugeru
So long!	またね！	mata ne!
Thank you!	ありがとう！	arigatō!
Thank you very much!	どうもありがとう！	dōmo arigatō!

You're welcome	どういたしまして	dōitashimashite
Don't mention it!	礼なんていいよ	rei nante ī yo
It was nothing	どういたしまして	dōitashimashite
Excuse me! (fam.)	失礼！	shitsurei!
Excuse me! (form.)	失礼致します！	shitsurei itashi masu!
to excuse (forgive)	許す	yurusu
to apologize (vi)	謝る	ayamaru
My apologies	おわび致します！	owabi itashi masu!
I'm sorry!	ごめんなさい！	gomennasai!
to forgive (vt)	許す	yurusu
It's okay!	大丈夫です！	daijōbu desu!
please (adv)	お願い	onegai
Don't forget!	忘れないで！	wasure nai de!
Certainly!	もちろん！	mochiron!
Of course not!	そんなことないよ！	sonna koto nai yo!
Okay! (I agree)	オーケー！	ōkē!
That's enough!	もう十分だ！	mō jūbun da!

3. How to address

Excuse me!	すみません、…	sumimasen , …
mister, sir	…さん	…san
ma'am	…さん	…san
miss	…さん	…san
young man	…さん	…san
young man (little boy)	…ちゃん	…chan
miss (little girl)	…ちゃん	…chan

4. Cardinal numbers. Part 1

0 zero	ゼロ	zero
1 one	一	ichi
2 two	二	ni
3 three	三	san
4 four	四	yon
5 five	五	go
6 six	六	roku
7 seven	七	nana
8 eight	八	hachi
9 nine	九	kyū

10 ten	十	jū
11 eleven	十一	jū ichi
12 twelve	十二	jū ni
13 thirteen	十三	jū san
14 fourteen	十四	jū yon
15 fifteen	十五	jū go
16 sixteen	十六	jū roku
17 seventeen	十七	jū shichi
18 eighteen	十八	jū hachi
19 nineteen	十九	jū kyū
20 twenty	二十	ni jū
21 twenty-one	二十一	ni jū ichi
22 twenty-two	二十二	ni jū ni
23 twenty-three	二十三	ni jū san
30 thirty	三十	san jū
31 thirty-one	三一	san jū ichi
32 thirty-two	三二	san jū ni
33 thirty-three	三三	san jū san
40 forty	四十	yon jū
41 forty-one	四一	yon jū ichi
42 forty-two	四二	yon jū ni
43 forty-three	四三	yon jū san
50 fifty	五十	go jū
51 fifty-one	五十一	go jū ichi
52 fifty-two	五十二	go jū ni
53 fifty-three	五十三	go jū san
60 sixty	六十	roku jū
61 sixty-one	六十一	roku jū ichi
62 sixty-two	六十二	roku jū ni
63 sixty-three	六十三	roku jū san
70 seventy	七十	nana jū
71 seventy-one	七十一	nana jū ichi
72 seventy-two	七十二	nana jū ni
73 seventy-three	七十三	nana jū san
80 eighty	八十	hachi jū
81 eighty-one	八十一	hachi jū ichi
82 eighty-two	八十二	hachi jū ni
83 eighty-three	八十三	hachi jū san
90 ninety	九十	kyū jū
91 ninety-one	九十一	kyū jū ichi
92 ninety-two	九十二	kyū jū ni
93 ninety-three	九十三	kyū jū san

5. Cardinal numbers. Part 2

100 one hundred	百	hyaku
200 two hundred	二百	ni hyaku
300 three hundred	三百	san byaku
400 four hundred	四百	yon hyaku
500 five hundred	五百	go hyaku
600 six hundred	六百	roppyaku
700 seven hundred	七百	nana hyaku
800 eight hundred	八百	happyaku
900 nine hundred	九百	kyū hyaku
1000 one thousand	千	sen
2000 two thousand	二千	nisen
3000 three thousand	三千	sanzen
10000 ten thousand	一万	ichiman
one hundred thousand	10万	jyūman
million	百万	hyakuman
billion	十億	jūoku

6. Ordinal numbers

first (adj)	第一の	dai ichi no
second (adj)	第二の	dai ni no
third (adj)	第三の	dai san no
fourth (adj)	第四の	dai yon no
fifth (adj)	第五の	dai go no
sixth (adj)	第六の	dai roku no
seventh (adj)	第七の	dai nana no
eighth (adj)	第八の	dai hachi no
ninth (adj)	第九の	dai kyū no
tenth (adj)	第十の	dai jū no

7. Numbers. Fractions

fraction	分数	bunsū
one half	2分の1	ni bunno ichi
one third	3分の1	san bunno ichi
one quarter	4分の1	yon bunno ichi
one eighth	8分の1	hachi bunno ichi
one tenth	10分の1	jyū bunno ichi
two thirds	3分の2	san bunno ni
three quarters	4分の3	yon bunno san

8. Numbers. Basic operations

subtraction	引き算	hikizan
to subtract (vi, vt)	引き算する	hikizan suru
division	割り算	warizan
to divide (vt)	割る	wareru
addition	加算	kasan
to add up (vt)	加算する	kasan suru
to add (vi, vt)	足す	tasu
multiplication	掛け算	kakezan
to multiply (vt)	掛ける	kakeru

9. Numbers. Miscellaneous

digit, figure	桁数	keta sū
number	数字	sūji
numeral	数詞	sūshi
minus sign	負号	fugō
plus sign	正符号	sei fugō
formula	公式	kōshiki
calculation	計算	keisan
to count (vt)	計算する	keisan suru
to count up	数える	kazoeru
to compare (vt)	比較する	hikaku suru
How much?	いくら？	ikura ?
How much?	いくら？	ikura ?
How many?	いくつ？	ikutsu ?
sum, total	合計	gōkei
result	結果	kekka
remainder	剰余、余り	jōyo, amari
a few …	少数の	shōsū no
few, little (adv)	少し	sukoshi
the rest	残り	nokori
one and a half	1,5	ittengo
dozen	ダース	dāsu
in half (adv)	半分に	hanbun ni
equally (evenly)	均等に	kintō ni
half	半分	hanbun
time (three ~s)	回	kai

10. The most important verbs. Part 1

to advise (vt)	助言する	jogen suru
to agree (say yes)	同意する	dōi suru

to answer (vi, vt)	回答する	kaitō suru
to apologize (vi)	謝る	ayamaru
to arrive (vi)	到着する	tōchaku suru
to ask (~ oneself)	問う	tō
to ask (~ sb to do sth)	頼む	tanomu
to be (vi)	ある	aru
to be afraid	怖がる	kowagaru
to be hungry	腹をすかす	hara wo sukasu
to be interested in …	…に興味がある	… ni kyōmi ga aru
to be needed	必要である	hitsuyō de aru
to be surprised	驚く	odoroku
to be thirsty	喉が渇く	nodo ga kawaku
to begin (vt)	始める	hajimeru
to belong to …	所有物である	shoyū butsu de aru
to boast (vi)	自慢する	jiman suru
to break (split into pieces)	折る、壊す	oru, kowasu
to call (for help)	求める	motomeru
can (v aux)	できる	dekiru
to catch (vt)	捕らえる	toraeru
to change (vt)	変える	kaeru
to choose (select)	選択する	sentaku suru
to come down	下りる	oriru
to come in (enter)	入る	hairu
to compare (vt)	比較する	hikaku suru
to complain (vi, vt)	不平を言う	fuhei wo iu
to confuse (mix up)	混同する	kondō suru
to continue (vt)	続ける	tsuzukeru
to control (vt)	管制する	kansei suru
to cook (dinner)	料理をする	ryōri wo suru
to cost (vt)	かかる	kakaru
to count (add up)	計算する	keisan suru
to count on …	…を頼りにする	… wo tayori ni suru
to create (vt)	創造する	sōzō suru
to cry (weep)	泣く	naku

11. The most important verbs. Part 2

to deceive (vi, vt)	だます	damasu
to decorate (tree, street)	飾る	kazaru
to defend (a country, etc.)	防衛する	bōei suru
to demand (request firmly)	要求する	yōkyū suru
to dig (vt)	掘る	horu
to discuss (vt)	討議する	tōgi suru

to do (vt)	する	suru
to doubt (have doubts)	疑う	utagau
to drop (let fall)	落とす	otosu
to excuse (forgive)	許す	yurusu
to exist (vi)	存在する	sonzai suru
to expect (foresee)	見越す	mikosu
to explain (vt)	説明する	setsumei suru
to fall (vi)	落ちる	ochiru
to find (vt)	見つける	mitsukeru
to finish (vt)	終える	oeru
to fly (vi)	飛ぶ	tobu
to follow ... (come after)	…について行く	... ni tsuiteiku
to forget (vi, vt)	忘れる	wasureru
to forgive (vt)	許す	yurusu
to give (vt)	手渡す	tewatasu
to give a hint	暗示する	anji suru
to go (on foot)	行く	iku
to go for a swim	海水浴をする	kaisuiyoku wo suru
to go out (from ...)	出る	deru
to guess right	言い当てる	īateru
to have (vt)	持つ	motsu
to have breakfast	朝食をとる	chōshoku wo toru
to have dinner	夕食をとる	yūshoku wo toru
to have lunch	昼食をとる	chūshoku wo toru
to hear (vt)	聞く	kiku
to help (vt)	手伝う	tetsudau
to hide (vt)	隠す	kakusu
to hope (vi, vt)	希望する	kibō suru
to hunt (vi, vt)	狩る	karu
to hurry (vi)	急ぐ	isogu

12. The most important verbs. Part 3

to inform (vt)	知らせる	shiraseru
to insist (vi, vt)	主張する	shuchō suru
to insult (vt)	侮辱する	bujoku suru
to invite (vt)	招待する	shōtai suru
to joke (vi)	冗談を言う	jōdan wo iu
to keep (vt)	保つ	tamotsu
to keep silent	沈黙を守る	chinmoku wo mamoru
to kill (vt)	殺す	korosu
to know (sb)	知っている	shitte iru
to know (sth)	知る	shiru

to laugh (vi)	笑う	warau
to liberate (city, etc.)	解放する	kaihō suru
to like (I like ...)	好む	konomu
to look for ... (search)	探す	sagasu
to love (sb)	愛する	aisuru
to make a mistake	誤りをする	ayamari wo suru
to manage, to run	管理する	kanri suru
to mean (signify)	意味する	imi suru
to mention (talk about)	言及する	genkyū suru
to miss (school, etc.)	欠席する	kesseki suru
to notice (see)	見掛ける	mikakeru
to object (vi, vt)	反対する	hantai suru
to observe (see)	監視する	kanshi suru
to open (vt)	開ける	akeru
to order (meal, etc.)	注文する	chūmon suru
to order (mil.)	命令する	meirei suru
to own (possess)	所有する	shoyū suru
to participate (vi)	参加する	sanka suru
to pay (vi, vt)	払う	harau
to permit (vt)	許可する	kyoka suru
to plan (vt)	計画する	keikaku suru
to play (children)	遊ぶ	asobu
to pray (vi, vt)	祈る	inoru
to prefer (vt)	好む	konomu
to promise (vt)	約束する	yakusoku suru
to pronounce (vt)	発音する	hatsuon suru
to propose (vt)	提案する	teian suru
to punish (vt)	罰する	bassuru
to read (vi, vt)	読む	yomu
to recommend (vt)	推薦する	suisen suru
to refuse (vi, vt)	拒絶する	kyozetsu suru
to regret (be sorry)	後悔する	kōkai suru
to rent (sth from sb)	借りる	kariru
to repeat (say again)	復唱する	fukushō suru
to reserve, to book	予約する	yoyaku suru
to run (vi)	走る	hashiru

13. The most important verbs. Part 4

to save (rescue)	救出する	kyūshutsu suru
to say (~ thank you)	言う	iu
to scold (vt)	叱る ［しかる］	shikaru
to see (vt)	見る	miru
to sell (vt)	売る	uru

to send (vt)	送る	okuru
to shoot (vi)	撃つ	utsu
to shout (vi)	叫ぶ	sakebu
to show (vt)	見せる	miseru
to sign (document)	署名する	shomei suru
to sit down (vi)	座る	suwaru
to smile (vi)	ほほえむ [微笑む]	hohoemu
to speak (vi, vt)	話す	hanasu
to steal (money, etc.)	盗む	nusumu
to stop (please ~ calling me)	止める	tomeru
to stop (for pause, etc.)	止まる	tomaru
to study (vt)	勉強する	benkyō suru
to swim (vi)	泳ぐ	oyogu
to take (vt)	取る	toru
to think (vi, vt)	思う	omō
to threaten (vt)	脅す	odosu
to touch (with hands)	触れる	fureru
to translate (vt)	翻訳する	honyaku suru
to trust (vt)	信用する	shinyō suru
to try (attempt)	試みる	kokoromiru
to turn (~ to the left)	曲がる	magaru
to underestimate (vt)	甘く見る	amaku miru
to understand (vt)	理解する	rikai suru
to unite (vt)	合体させる	gattai saseru
to wait (vt)	待つ	matsu
to want (wish, desire)	欲する	hossuru
to warn (vt)	警告する	keikoku suru
to work (vi)	働く	hataraku
to write (vt)	書く	kaku
to write down	書き留める	kakitomeru

14. Colors

color	色	iro
shade (tint)	色合い	iroai
hue	色相	shikisō
rainbow	虹	niji
white (adj)	白い	shiroi
black (adj)	黒い	kuroi
gray (adj)	灰色の	haīro no
green (adj)	緑の	midori no
yellow (adj)	黄色い	kīroi
red (adj)	赤い	akai

blue (adj)	青い	aoi
light blue (adj)	水色の	mizu iro no
pink (adj)	ピンクの	pinku no
orange (adj)	オレンジの	orenji no
violet (adj)	紫色の	murasaki iro no
brown (adj)	茶色の	chairo no
golden (adj)	金色の	kiniro no
silvery (adj)	銀色の	giniro no
beige (adj)	ベージュの	bēju no
cream (adj)	クリームの	kurīmu no
turquoise (adj)	ターコイズブルーの	tākoizuburū no
cherry red (adj)	チェリーレッドの	cherī reddo no
lilac (adj)	ライラックの	rairakku no
crimson (adj)	クリムゾンの	kurimuzon no
light (adj)	薄い	usui
dark (adj)	濃い	koi
bright, vivid (adj)	鮮やかな	azayaka na
colored (pencils)	色の	iro no
color (e.g., ~ film)	カラー…	karā…
black-and-white (adj)	白黒の	shirokuro no
plain (one-colored)	単色の	tanshoku no
multicolored (adj)	色とりどりの	irotoridori no

15. Questions

Who?	誰？	dare ?
What?	何？	nani ?
Where? (at, in)	どこに？	doko ni ?
Where (to)?	どちらへ？	dochira he ?
From where?	どこから？	doko kara ?
When?	いつ？	itsu ?
Why? (What for?)	なんで？	nande ?
Why? (reason)	どうして？	dōshite ?
What for?	何のために？	nan no tame ni ?
How? (in what way)	どうやって？	dō yatte?
What? (What kind of ...?)	どんな　？	donna?
Which?	どちらの…？	dochira no … ?
To whom?	誰に？	dare ni ?
About whom?	誰のこと？	dare no koto ?
About what?	何のこと？	nannokoto ?
With whom?	誰と？	dare to ?
How many?	いくつ？	ikutsu ?
How much?	いくら？	ikura ?
Whose?	誰のもの？	Dare no mono ?

16. Prepositions

with (accompanied by)	…と、…と共に	… to, totomoni
without	…なしで	… nashi de
to (indicating direction)	…へ	… he
about (talking ~ ...)	…について	… ni tsuite
before (in time)	…の前に	… no mae ni
in front of ...	…の正面に	… no shōmen ni
under (beneath, below)	下に	shita ni
above (over)	上側に	uwagawa ni
on (atop)	上に	ue ni
from (off, out of)	…から	… kara
of (made from)	…製の	… sei no
in (e.g., ~ ten minutes)	…で	… de
over (across the top of)	…を越えて	… wo koe te

17. Function words. Adverbs. Part 1

Where? (at, in)	どこに？	doko ni ?
here (adv)	ここで	kokode
there (adv)	そこで	sokode
somewhere (to be)	どこかで	doko ka de
nowhere (not anywhere)	どこにも	doko ni mo
by (near, beside)	近くで	chikaku de
by the window	窓辺に	mado beni
Where (to)?	どちらへ？	dochira he ?
here (e.g., come ~!)	こちらへ	kochira he
there (e.g., to go ~)	そこへ	soko he
from here (adv)	ここから	koko kara
from there (adv)	そこから	soko kara
close (adv)	そばに	soba ni
far (adv)	遠くに	tōku ni
near (e.g., ~ Paris)	近く	chikaku
nearby (adv)	近くに	chikaku ni
not far (adv)	遠くない	tōku nai
left (adj)	左の	hidari no
on the left	左に	hidari ni
to the left	左へ	hidari he
right (adj)	右の	migi no
on the right	右に	migi ni

to the right	右へ	migi he
in front (adv)	前に	mae ni
front (as adj)	前の	mae no
ahead (look ~)	前方へ	zenpō he

behind (adv)	後ろに	ushiro ni
from behind	後ろから	ushiro kara
back (towards the rear)	後ろへ	ushiro he

| middle | 中央 | chūō |
| in the middle | 中央に | chūō ni |

at the side	側面から	sokumen kara
everywhere (adv)	どこでも	doko demo
around (in all directions)	…の周りを	… no mawari wo

from inside	中から	naka kara
somewhere (to go)	どこかへ	dokoka he
straight (directly)	真っ直ぐに	massugu ni
back (e.g., come ~)	戻って	modotte

| from anywhere | どこからでも | doko kara demo |
| from somewhere | どこからか | doko kara ka |

firstly (adv)	第一に	dai ichi ni
secondly (adv)	第二に	dai ni ni
thirdly (adv)	第三に	dai san ni

suddenly (adv)	急に	kyū ni
at first (adv)	初めは	hajime wa
for the first time	初めて	hajimete
long before …	…かなり前に	…kanari mae ni
anew (over again)	新たに	arata ni
for good (adv)	永遠に	eien ni

never (adv)	一度も	ichi do mo
again (adv)	再び	futatabi
now (adv)	今	ima
often (adv)	よく	yoku
then (adv)	あのとき	ano toki
urgently (quickly)	至急に	shikyū ni
usually (adv)	普通は	futsū wa

by the way, …	ところで、…	tokorode, …
possible (that is ~)	可能な	kanō na
probably (adv)	恐らく［おそらく］	osoraku
maybe (adv)	ことによると	kotoni yoru to
besides …	それに	soreni
that's why …	従って	shitagatte
in spite of …	…にもかかわらず	… ni mo kakawara zu
thanks to …	…のおかげで	… no okage de
what (pron.)	何	nani

that (conj.)	…ということ	… toyuu koto
something	何か	nani ka
anything (something)	何か	nani ka
nothing	何もない	nani mo nai
who (pron.)	誰	dare
someone	ある人	aru hito
somebody	誰か	dare ka
nobody	誰も…ない	dare mo … nai
nowhere (a voyage to ~)	どこへも	doko he mo
nobody's	誰の…でもない	dare no … de mo nai
somebody's	誰かの	dare ka no
so (I'm ~ glad)	とても	totemo
also (as well)	また	mata
too (as well)	も	mo

18. Function words. Adverbs. Part 2

Why?	どうして？	dōshite ?
for some reason	なぜか ［何故か］	naze ka
because …	なぜなら	nazenara
for some purpose	何らかの理由で	nanrakano riyū de
and	と	to
or	または	matawa
but	でも	demo
for (e.g., ~ me)	…のために	… no tame ni
too (~ many people)	…すぎる	… sugiru
only (exclusively)	もっぱら	moppara
exactly (adv)	正確に	seikaku ni
about (more or less)	約	yaku
approximately (adv)	おおよそ	ōyoso
approximate (adj)	おおよその	ōyosono
almost (adv)	ほとんど	hotondo
the rest	残り	nokori
the other (second)	もう一方の	mōippōno
other (different)	他の	hokano
each (adj)	各	kaku
any (no matter which)	どれでも	dore demo
many (adv)	多くの	ōku no
much (adv)	多量の	taryō no
many people	多くの人々	ōku no hitobito
all (everyone)	あらゆる人	arayuru hito
in return for …	…の返礼として	… no henrei toshite
in exchange (adv)	引き換えに	hikikae ni

by hand (made)	手で	te de
hardly (negative opinion)	ほとんど…ない	hotondo … nai
probably (adv)	恐らく［おそらく］	osoraku
on purpose (adv)	わざと	wazato
by accident (adv)	偶然に	gūzen ni
very (adv)	非常に	hijō ni
for example (adv)	例えば	tatoeba
between	間	kan
among	…の間で	… no мade
so much (such a lot)	たくさん	takusan
especially (adv)	特に	tokuni

Basic concepts. Part 2

19. Weekdays

Monday	月曜日	getsuyōbi
Tuesday	火曜日	kayōbi
Wednesday	水曜日	suiyōbi
Thursday	木曜日	mokuyōbi
Friday	金曜日	kinyōbi
Saturday	土曜日	doyōbi
Sunday	日曜日	nichiyōbi
today (adv)	今日	kyō
tomorrow (adv)	明日	ashita
the day after tomorrow	明後日 ［あさって］	asatte
yesterday (adv)	昨日	kinō
the day before yesterday	一昨日 ［おととい］	ototoi
day	日	nichi
working day	営業日	eigyōbi
public holiday	公休	kōkyū
day off	休み	yasumi
weekend	週末	shūmatsu
all day long	一日中	ichi nichi chū
next day (adv)	翌日	yokujitsu
two days ago	2日前に	futsu ka mae ni
the day before	その前日に	sono zenjitsu ni
daily (adj)	毎日の	mainichi no
every day (adv)	毎日	mainichi
week	週	shū
last week (adv)	先週	senshū
next week (adv)	来週	raishū
weekly (adj)	毎週の	maishū no
every week (adv)	毎週	maishū
twice a week	週に2回	shūni nikai
every Tuesday	毎週火曜日	maishū kayōbi

20. Hours. Day and night

morning	朝	asa
in the morning	朝に	asa ni
noon, midday	正午	shōgo

in the afternoon	午後に	gogo ni
evening	夕方	yūgata
in the evening	夕方に	yūgata ni
night	夜	yoru
at night	夜に	yoru ni
midnight	真夜中	mayonaka
second	秒	byō
minute	分	fun, pun
hour	時間	jikan
half an hour	30分	san jū fun
quarter of an hour	15分	jū go fun
fifteen minutes	15分	jū go fun
24 hours	一昼夜	icchūya
sunrise	日の出	hinode
dawn	夜明け	yoake
early morning	早朝	sōchō
sunset	夕日	yūhi
early in the morning	早朝に	sōchō ni
this morning	今朝	kesa
tomorrow morning	明日の朝	ashita no asa
this afternoon	今日の午後	kyō no gogo
in the afternoon	午後	gogo
tomorrow afternoon	明日の午後	ashita no gogo
tonight (this evening)	今夜	konya
tomorrow night	明日の夜	ashita no yoru
at 3 o'clock sharp	3時ちょうどに	sanji chōdo ni
about 4 o'clock	4時頃	yoji goro
by 12 o'clock	12時までに	jūniji made ni
in 20 minutes	20分後	nijuppungo
in an hour	一時間後	ichi jikan go
on time (adv)	予定通りに	yotei dōri ni
a quarter of ...	…時15分	… ji jyūgo fun
within an hour	1時間で	ichi jikan de
every 15 minutes	15分ごとに	jyūgo fun goto ni
round the clock	昼も夜も	hiru mo yoru mo

21. Months. Seasons

January	一月	ichigatsu
February	二月	nigatsu
March	三月	sangatsu
April	四月	shigatsu

May	五月	gogatsu
June	六月	rokugatsu
July	七月	shichigatsu
August	八月	hachigatsu
September	九月	kugatsu
October	十月	jūgatsu
November	十一月	jūichigatsu
December	十二月	jūnigatsu
spring	春	haru
in spring	春に	haru ni
spring (as adj)	春の	haru no
summer	夏	natsu
in summer	夏に	natsu ni
summer (as adj)	夏の	natsu no
fall	秋	aki
in fall	秋に	aki ni
fall (as adj)	秋の	aki no
winter	冬	fuyu
in winter	冬に	fuyu ni
winter (as adj)	冬の	fuyu no
month	月	tsuki
this month	今月	kongetsu
next month	来月	raigetsu
last month	先月	sengetsu
a month ago	一ヶ月前	ichi kagetsu mae
in a month	一ヶ月後	ichi kagetsu go
in two months	二ヶ月後	ni kagetsu go
the whole month	丸一ヶ月	maru ichi kagetsu
all month long	一ヶ月間ずっと	ichi kagetsu kan zutto
monthly (~ magazine)	月刊の	gekkan no
monthly (adv)	毎月	maitsuki
every month	月1回	tsuki ichi kai
twice a month	月に2回	tsuki ni ni kai
year	年	nen
this year	今年	kotoshi
next year	来年	rainen
last year	去年	kyonen
a year ago	一年前	ichi nen mae
in a year	一年後	ichi nen go
in two years	二年後	ni nen go
the whole year	丸一年	maru ichi nen
all year long	通年	tsūnen

every year	毎年	maitoshi
annual (adj)	毎年の	maitoshi no
annually (adv)	年1回	toshi ichi kai
4 times a year	年に4回	

date (e.g., today's ~)	日付	hizuke
date (e.g., ~ of birth)	年月日	nengappi
calendar	カレンダー	karendā

| half a year | 半年 | hantoshi |
| six months | 6ヶ月 | |

| season (summer, etc.) | 季節 | kisetsu |
| century | 世紀 | seiki |

22. Units of measurement

weight	重さ	omo sa
length	長さ	naga sa
width	幅	haba
height	高さ	taka sa
depth	深さ	fuka sa
volume	体積	taiseki
area	面積	menseki

gram	グラム	guramu
milligram	ミリグラム	miriguramu
kilogram	キログラム	kiroguramu
ton	トン	ton
pound	ポンド	pondo
ounce	オンス	onsu

meter	メートル	mētoru
millimeter	ミリメートル	mirimētoru
centimeter	センチメートル	senchimētoru
kilometer	キロメートル	kiromētoru
mile	マイル	mairu

inch	インチ	inchi
foot	フィート	fīto
yard	ヤード	yādo

| square meter | 平方メートル | heihō mētoru |
| hectare | ヘクタール | hekutāru |

liter	リットル	rittoru
degree	度	do
volt	ボルト	boruto
ampere	アンペア	anpea

horsepower	馬力	bariki
quantity	数量	sūryō
a little bit of ...	少し	sukoshi
half	半分	hanbun
dozen	ダース	dāsu
piece (item)	一個	ikko
size	大きさ	ōki sa
scale (map ~)	縮尺	shukushaku
minimal (adj)	極小の	kyokushō no
the smallest (adj)	最小の	saishō no
medium (adj)	中位の	chūi no
maximal (adj)	極大の	kyokudai no
the largest (adj)	最大の	saidai no

23. Containers

jar (glass)	ジャー、瓶	jā, bin
can	缶	kan
bucket	バケツ	baketsu
barrel	樽	taru
basin (for washing)	たらい [盥]	tarai
tank (for liquid, gas)	タンク	tanku
hip flask	スキットル	sukittoru
jerrycan	ジェリカン	jerikan
cistern (tank)	積荷タンク	tsumini tanku
mug	マグカップ	magukappu
cup (of coffee, etc.)	カップ	kappu
saucer	ソーサー	sōsā
glass (tumbler)	ガラスのコップ	garasu no koppu
wineglass	ワイングラス	wain gurasu
saucepan	両手鍋	ryō tenabe
bottle (~ of wine)	ボトル	botoru
neck (of the bottle)	ネック	nekku
carafe	デキャンター	dekyanta
pitcher (earthenware)	水差し	mizusashi
vessel (container)	器	utsuwa
pot (crock)	鉢	hachi
vase	花瓶	kabin
bottle (~ of perfume)	瓶	bin
vial, small bottle	バイアル	bai aru
tube (of toothpaste)	チューブ	chūbu
sack (bag)	南京袋	nankinbukuro
bag (paper ~, plastic ~)	袋	fukuro

pack (of cigarettes, etc.)	箱	hako
box (e.g., shoebox)	箱	hako
crate	木箱	ki bako
basket	かご [籠]	kago

HUMAN BEING

Human being. The body

24. Head

head	頭	atama
face	顔	kao
nose	鼻	hana
mouth	口	kuchi
eye	眼	me
eyes	両眼	ryōgan
pupil	瞳	hitomi
eyebrow	眉	mayu
eyelash	まつげ	matsuge
eyelid	まぶた	mabuta
tongue	舌	shita
tooth	歯	ha
lips	唇	kuchibiru
cheekbones	頬骨	hōbone
gum	歯茎	haguki
palate	口蓋	kōgai
nostrils	鼻孔	bikō
chin	あご（頤）	ago
jaw	顎	ago
cheek	頬	hō
forehead	額	hitai
temple	こめかみ	komekami
ear	耳	mimi
back of the head	後頭部	kōtōbu
neck	首	kubi
throat	喉	nodo
hair	髪の毛	kaminoke
hairstyle	髪形	kamigata
haircut	髪型	kamigata
wig	かつら	katsura
mustache	口ひげ	kuchihige
beard	あごひげ	agohige
to have (a beard, etc.)	生やしている	hayashi te iru

| braid | 三つ編み | mitsu ami |
| sideburns | もみあげ | momiage |

red-haired (adj)	赤毛の	akage no
gray (hair)	白髪の	hakuhatsu no
bald (adj)	はげ頭の	hageatama no
bald patch	はげた部分	hage ta bubun

| ponytail | ポニーテール | ponītēru |
| bangs | 前髪 | maegami |

25. Human body

| hand | 手 | te |
| arm | 腕 | ude |

finger	指	yubi
toe	つま先	tsumasaki
thumb	親指	oyayubi
little finger	小指	koyubi
nail	爪	tsume

fist	拳	kobushi
palm	手のひら	tenohira
wrist	手首	tekubi
forearm	前腕	zen wan
elbow	肘	hiji
shoulder	肩	kata

leg	足［脚］	ashi
foot	足	ashi
knee	膝	hiza
calf (part of leg)	ふくらはぎ	fuku ra hagi
hip	腰	koshi
heel	かかと［踵］	kakato

body	身体	shintai
stomach	腹	hara
chest	胸	mune
breast	乳房	chibusa
flank	脇腹	wakibara
back	背中	senaka
lower back	腰背部	yōwa ibu
waist	腰	koshi

navel	へそ［臍］	heso
buttocks	臀部	denbu
bottom	尻	shiri
beauty mark	美人ぼくろ	bijinbokuro
birthmark	母斑	bohan

| tattoo | タトゥー | tatū |
| scar | 傷跡 | kizuato |

Clothing & Accessories

26. Outerwear. Coats

clothes	洋服	yōfuku
outer clothes	上着	uwagi
winter clothes	冬服	fuyu fuku
overcoat	オーバーコート	ōbā kōto
fur coat	毛皮のコート	kegawa no kōto
fur jacket	毛皮のジャケット	kegawa no jaketto
down coat	ダウンコート	daun kōto
jacket (e.g., leather ~)	ジャケット	jaketto
raincoat	レインコート	reinkōto
waterproof (adj)	防水の	bōsui no

27. Men's & women's clothing

shirt	ワイシャツ	waishatsu
pants	ズボン	zubon
jeans	ジーンズ	jīnzu
jacket (of man's suit)	ジャケット	jaketto
suit	背広	sebiro
dress (frock)	ドレス	doresu
skirt	スカート	sukāto
blouse	ブラウス	burausu
knitted jacket	ニットジャケット	nitto jaketto
jacket (of woman's suit)	ジャケット	jaketto
T-shirt	Tシャツ	tīshatsu
shorts (short trousers)	半ズボン	han zubon
tracksuit	トラックスーツ	torakku sūtsu
bathrobe	バスローブ	basurōbu
pajamas	パジャマ	pajama
sweater	セーター	sētā
pullover	プルオーバー	puruōbā
vest	ベスト	besuto
tailcoat	燕尾服	enbifuku
tuxedo	タキシード	takishīdo
uniform	制服	seifuku

workwear	作業服	sagyō fuku
overalls	オーバーオール	ōbā ōru
coat (e.g., doctor's smock)	コート	kōto

28. Clothing. Underwear

underwear	下着	shitagi
boxers	ボクサーパンツ	bokusā pantsu
panties	パンティー	pantī
undershirt (A-shirt)	タンクトップ	tanku toppu
socks	靴下	kutsushita

nightgown	ネグリジェ	negurije
bra	ブラジャー	burajā
knee highs	ニーソックス	nīsokkusu
tights	パンティストッキング	pantī sutokkingu
stockings (thigh highs)	ストッキング	sutokkingu
bathing suit	水着	mizugi

29. Headwear

hat	帽子	bōshi
fedora	フェドーラ帽	fedōra bō
baseball cap	野球帽	yakyū bō
flatcap	ハンチング帽	hanchingu bō

beret	ベレー帽	berē bō
hood	フード	fūdo
panama hat	パナマ帽	panama bō
knitted hat	ニット帽	nitto bō

headscarf	ヘッドスカーフ	heddo sukāfu
women's hat	婦人帽子	fujin bōshi

hard hat	安全ヘルメット	anzen herumetto
garrison cap	略帽	rya ku bō
helmet	ヘルメット	herumetto

derby	山高帽	yamataka bō
top hat	シルクハット	shiruku hatto

30. Footwear

footwear	靴	kutsu
ankle boots	アンクルブーツ	ankuru būtsu
shoes (low-heeled ~)	パンプス	panpusu

boots (cowboy ~)	ブーツ	būtsu
slippers	スリッパ	surippa
tennis shoes	テニスシューズ	tenisu shūzu
sneakers	スニーカー	sunīkā
sandals	サンダル	sandaru
cobbler	靴修理屋	kutsu shūri ya
heel	かかと [踵]	kakato
pair (of shoes)	靴一足	kutsu issoku
shoestring	靴ひも	kutsu himo
to lace (vt)	靴ひもを結ぶ	kutsu himo wo musubu
shoehorn	靴べら	kutsubera
shoe polish	靴クリーム	kutsu kurīmu

31. Personal accessories

gloves	手袋	tebukuro
mittens	ミトン	miton
scarf (muffler)	マフラー	mafurā
glasses	めがね [眼鏡]	megane
frame (eyeglass ~)	めがねのふち	megane no fuchi
umbrella	傘	kasa
walking stick	杖	tsue
hairbrush	ヘアブラシ	hea burashi
fan	扇子	sensu
necktie	ネクタイ	nekutai
bow tie	蝶ネクタイ	chō nekutai
suspenders	サスペンダー	sasupendā
handkerchief	ハンカチ	hankachi
comb	くし [櫛]	kushi
barrette	髪留め	kami tome
hairpin	ヘアピン	hea pin
buckle	バックル	bakkuru
belt	ベルト	beruto
shoulder strap	ショルダーベルト	shorudā beruto
bag (handbag)	バッグ	baggu
purse	ハンドバッグ	hando baggu
backpack	バックパック	bakku pakku

32. Clothing. Miscellaneous

| fashion | ファッション | fasshon |
| in vogue (adj) | 流行の | ryūkō no |

fashion designer	ファッションデザイナー	fasshon dezainā
collar	襟	eri
pocket	ポケット	poketto
pocket (as adj)	ポケットの	poketto no
sleeve	袖	sode
hanging loop	ハンガーループ	hangā rūpu
fly (on trousers)	ズボンのファスナー	zubon no fasunā
zipper (fastener)	チャック	chakku
fastener	ファスナー	fasunā
button	ボタン	botan
buttonhole	ボタンの穴	botan no ana
to come off (ab. button)	取れる	toreru
to sew (vi, vt)	縫う	nū
to embroider (vi, vt)	刺繍する	shishū suru
embroidery	刺繍	shishū
sewing needle	縫い針	nui bari
thread	糸	ito
seam	縫い目	nuime
to get dirty (vi)	汚れる	yogoreru
stain (mark, spot)	染み	shimi
to crease, crumple (vi)	しわになる	shiwa ni naru
to tear (vt)	引き裂く	hikisaku
clothes moth	コイガ	koi ga

33. Personal care. Cosmetics

toothpaste	歯磨き粉	hamigakiko
toothbrush	歯ブラシ	haburashi
to brush one's teeth	歯を磨く	ha wo migaku
razor	カミソリ [剃刀]	kamisori
shaving cream	シェービングクリーム	shēbingu kurīmu
to shave (vi)	ひげを剃る	hige wo soru
soap	せっけん [石鹸]	sekken
shampoo	シャンプー	shanpū
scissors	はさみ	hasami
nail file	爪やすり	tsume yasuri
nail clippers	爪切り	tsume giri
tweezers	ピンセット	pinsetto
cosmetics	化粧品	keshō hin
face mask	フェイスパック	feisu pakku
manicure	マニキュア	manikyua
to have a manicure	マニキュアをしてもらう	manikyua wo shi te morau
pedicure	ペディキュア	pedikyua

make-up bag	化粧ポーチ	keshō pōchi
face powder	フェイスパウダー	feisu pauda
powder compact	ファンデーション	fandēshon
blusher	チーク	chīku
perfume (bottled)	香水	kōsui
toilet water (perfume)	オードトワレ	ōdotoware
lotion	ローション	rō shon
cologne	オーデコロン	ōdekoron
eyeshadow	アイシャドウ	aishadō
eyeliner	アイライナー	airainā
mascara	マスカラ	masukara
lipstick	口紅	kuchibeni
nail polish, enamel	ネイルポリッシュ	neiru porisshu
hair spray	ヘアスプレー	hea supurē
deodorant	デオドラント	deodoranto
cream	クリーム	kurīmu
face cream	フェイスクリーム	feisu kurīmu
hand cream	ハンドクリーム	hando kurīmu
anti-wrinkle cream	しわ取りクリーム	shiwa tori kurīmu
day cream	昼用クリーム	hiruyō kurīmu
night cream	夜用クリーム	yoruyō kurīmu
day (as adj)	昼用…	hiruyō …
night (as adj)	夜用…	yoruyō …
tampon	タンポン	tanpon
toilet paper	トイレットペーパー	toiretto pēpā
hair dryer	ヘアドライヤー	hea doraiyā

34. Watches. Clocks

watch (wristwatch)	時計	tokei
dial	ダイヤル	daiyaru
hand (of clock, watch)	針	hari
metal watch band	金属ベルト	kinzoku beruto
watch strap	腕時計バンド	udedokei bando
battery	電池	denchi
to be dead (battery)	切れる	kireru
to change a battery	電池を交換する	denchi wo kōkan suru
to run fast	進んでいる	susundeiru
to run slow	遅れている	okureteiru
wall clock	掛け時計	kakedokei
hourglass	砂時計	sunadokei
sundial	日時計	hidokei
alarm clock	目覚まし時計	mezamashi dokei

| watchmaker | 時計職人 | tokei shokunin |
| to repair (vt) | 修理する | shūri suru |

Food. Nutricion

meat	肉	niku
chicken	鶏	niwatori
young chicken	若鶏	wakadori
duck	ダック	dakku
goose	ガチョウ	gachō
game	獲物	emono
turkey	七面鳥	shichimenchuō
pork	豚肉	buta niku
veal	子牛肉	kōshi niku
lamb	子羊肉	kohitsuji niku
beef	牛肉	gyū niku
rabbit	兎肉	usagi niku
sausage (salami, etc.)	ソーセージ	sōsēji
vienna sausage	ソーセージ	sōsēji
bacon	ベーコン	bēkon
ham	ハム	hamu
gammon (ham)	ガモン	gamon
pâté	パテ	pate
liver	レバー	rebā
lard	ラード	rādo
ground beef	挽肉	hikiniku
tongue	タン	tan
egg	卵	tamago
eggs	卵	tamago
egg white	卵の白身	tamago no shiromi
egg yolk	卵の黄身	tamago no kimi
fish	魚	sakana
seafood	魚介	gyokai
caviar	キャビア	kyabia
crab	カニ [蟹]	kani
shrimp	エビ	ebi
oyster	カキ [牡蠣]	kaki
spiny lobster	伊勢エビ	ise ebi
octopus	タコ	tako
squid	イカ	ika
sturgeon	チョウザメ	chōzame

salmon	サケ [鮭]	sake
halibut	ハリバット	haribatto
cod	タラ [鱈]	tara
mackerel	サバ [鯖]	saba
tuna	マグロ [鮪]	maguro
eel	ウナギ [鰻]	unagi
trout	マス [鱒]	masu
sardine	イワシ	iwashi
pike	カワカマス	kawakamasu
herring	ニシン	nishin
bread	パン	pan
cheese	チーズ	chīzu
sugar	砂糖	satō
salt	塩	shio
rice	米	kome
pasta	パスタ	pasuta
noodles	麺	men
butter	バター	batā
vegetable oil	植物油	shokubutsu yu
sunflower oil	ひまわり油	himawari yu
margarine	マーガリン	māgarin
olives	オリーブ	orību
olive oil	オリーブ油	orību yu
milk	乳、ミルク	nyū, miruku
condensed milk	練乳	rennyū
yogurt	ヨーグルト	yōguruto
sour cream	サワークリーム	sawā kurīmu
cream (of milk)	クリーム	kurīmu
mayonnaise	マヨネーズ	mayonēzu
buttercream	バタークリーム	batā kurīmu
cereal grain (wheat, etc.)	穀物	kokumotsu
flour	小麦粉	komugiko
canned food	缶詰	kanzume
cornflakes	コーンフレーク	kōn furēku
honey	蜂蜜	hachimitsu
jam	ジャム	jamu
chewing gum	チューインガム	chūin gamu

36. Drinks

water	水	mizu
drinking water	飲用水	inyō sui
mineral water	ミネラルウォーター	mineraru wōtā

still (adj)	無炭酸の	mu tansan no
carbonated (adj)	炭酸の	tansan no
sparkling (adj)	発泡性の	happō sei no
ice	氷	kōri
with ice	氷入りの	kōri iri no
non-alcoholic (adj)	ノンアルコールの	non arukŌru no
soft drink	炭酸飲料	tansan inryō
cool soft drink	清涼飲料水	seiryōinryōsui
lemonade	レモネード	remonēdo
liquor	アルコール	arukōru
wine	ワイン	wain
white wine	白ワイン	shiro wain
red wine	赤ワイン	aka wain
liqueur	リキュール	rikyūru
champagne	シャンパン	shanpan
vermouth	ベルモット	berumotto
whisky	ウイスキー	uisukī
vodka	ウォッカ	wokka
gin	ジン	jin
cognac	コニャック	konyakku
rum	ラム酒	ramu shu
coffee	コーヒー	kōhī
black coffee	ブラックコーヒー	burakku kōhī
coffee with milk	ミルク入りコーヒー	miruku iri kōhī
cappuccino	カプチーノ	kapuchīno
instant coffee	インスタントコーヒー	insutanto kōhī
milk	乳、ミルク	nyū, miruku
cocktail	カクテル	kakuteru
milk shake	ミルクセーキ	miruku sēki
juice	ジュース	jūsu
tomato juice	トマトジュース	tomato jūsu
orange juice	オレンジジュース	orenji jūsu
freshly squeezed juice	搾りたてのジュース	shibori tate no jūsu
beer	ビール	bīru
light beer	ライトビール	raito bīru
dark beer	黒ビール	kuro bīru
tea	茶	cha
black tea	紅茶	kō cha
green tea	緑茶	ryoku cha

37. Vegetables

vegetables	野菜	yasai
greens	青物	aomono
tomato	トマト	tomato
cucumber	きゅうり [胡瓜]	kyūri
carrot	ニンジン [人参]	ninjin
potato	ジャガイモ	jagaimo
onion	たまねぎ [玉葱]	tamanegi
garlic	ニンニク	ninniku
cabbage	キャベツ	kyabetsu
cauliflower	カリフラワー	karifurawā
Brussels sprouts	メキャベツ	mekyabetsu
broccoli	ブロッコリー	burokkorī
beetroot	テーブルビート	tēburu bīto
eggplant	ナス	nasu
zucchini	ズッキーニ	zukkīni
pumpkin	カボチャ	kabocha
turnip	カブ	kabu
parsley	パセリ	paseri
dill	ディル	diru
lettuce	レタス	retasu
celery	セロリ	serori
asparagus	アスパラガス	asuparagasu
spinach	ホウレンソウ	hōrensō
pea	エンドウ	endō
beans	豆類	mamerui
corn (maize)	トウモロコシ	tōmorokoshi
kidney bean	金時豆	kintoki mame
pepper	コショウ	koshō
radish	ハツカダイコン	hatsukadaikon
artichoke	アーティチョーク	ātichōku

38. Fruits. Nuts

fruit	果物	kudamono
apple	リンゴ	ringo
pear	洋梨	yōnashi
lemon	レモン	remon
orange	オレンジ	orenji
strawberry	イチゴ（苺）	ichigo
mandarin	マンダリン	mandarin
plum	プラム	puramu

peach	モモ ［桃］	momo
apricot	アンズ ［杏子］	anzu
raspberry	ラズベリー （木苺）	razuberī
pineapple	パイナップル	painappuru

banana	バナナ	banana
watermelon	スイカ	suika
grape	ブドウ ［葡萄］	budō
cherry	チェリー	cherī
sour cherry	サワー チェリー	sawā cherī
sweet cherry	スイート チェリー	suīto cherī
melon	メロン	meron

grapefruit	グレープフルーツ	gurēbu furūtsu
avocado	アボカド	abokado
papaya	パパイヤ	papaiya
mango	マンゴー	mangō
pomegranate	ザクロ	zakuro

redcurrant	フサスグリ	fusa suguri
blackcurrant	クロスグリ	kuro suguri
gooseberry	セイヨウスグリ	seiyō suguri
bilberry	ビルベリー	biruberī
blackberry	ブラックベリー	burakku berī

raisin	レーズン	rēzun
fig	イチジク	ichijiku
date	デーツ	dētsu

peanut	ピーナッツ	pīnattsu
almond	アーモンド	āmondo
walnut	クルミ （胡桃）	kurumi
hazelnut	ヘーゼルナッツ	hēzeru nattsu
coconut	ココナッツ	koko nattsu
pistachios	ピスタチオ	pisutachio

39. Bread. Candy

confectionery (pastry)	菓子類	kashi rui
bread	パン	pan
cookies	クッキー	kukkī

chocolate (n)	チョコレート	chokorēto
chocolate (as adj)	チョコレートの	chokorēto no
candy	キャンディー	kyandī
cake (e.g., cupcake)	ケーキ	kēki
cake (e.g., birthday ~)	ケーキ	kēki

| pie (e.g., apple ~) | パイ | pai |
| filling (for cake, pie) | フィリング | firingu |

whole fruit jam	ジャム	jamu
marmalade	マーマレード	māmarēdo
waffle	ワッフル	waffuru
ice-cream	アイスクリーム	aisukurīmu
pudding	プディング	pudingu

40. Cooked dishes

course, dish	料理	ryōri
cuisine	料理	ryōri
recipe	レシピ	reshipi
portion	一人前	ichi ninmae
salad	サラダ	sarada
soup	スープ	sūpu
clear soup (broth)	ブイヨン	buiyon
sandwich (bread)	サンドイッチ	sandoicchi
fried eggs	目玉焼き	medamayaki
cutlet (croquette)	クロケット	kuroketto
hamburger (beefburger)	ハンバーガー	hanbāgā
beefsteak	ビーフステーキ	bīfusutēki
stew	シチュー	shichū
side dish	付け合わせ	tsukeawase
spaghetti	スパゲッティ	supagetti
mashed potatoes	マッシュポテト	masshupoteto
pizza	ピザ	piza
porridge (oatmeal, etc.)	ポリッジ	porijji
omelet	オムレツ	omuretsu
boiled (e.g., ~ beef)	煮た	ni ta
smoked (adj)	薫製の	kunsei no
fried (adj)	揚げた	age ta
dried (adj)	干した	hoshi ta
frozen (adj)	冷凍の	reitō no
pickled (adj)	酢漬けの	suzuke no
sweet (sugary)	甘い	amai
salty (adj)	塩味の	shioaji no
cold (adj)	冷たい	tsumetai
hot (adj)	熱い	atsui
bitter (adj)	苦い	nigai
tasty (adj)	美味しい	oishī
to cook in boiling water	水で煮る	mizu de niru
to cook (dinner)	料理をする	ryōri wo suru
to fry (vt)	揚げる	ageru
to heat up (food)	温める	atatameru

to salt (vt)	塩をかける	shio wo kakeru
to pepper (vt)	コショウをかける	koshō wo kakeru
to grate (vt)	すりおろす	suri orosu
peel (n)	皮	kawa
to peel (vt)	皮をむく	kawa wo muku

41. Spices

salt	塩	shio
salty (adj)	塩味の	shioaji no
to salt (vt)	塩をかける	shio wo kakeru

black pepper	黒コショウ	kuro koshō
red pepper	赤唐辛子	aka tōgarashi
mustard	マスタード	masutādo
horseradish	セイヨウワサビ	seiyō wasabi

condiment	調味料	chōmiryō
spice	香辛料	kōshinryō
sauce	ソース	sōsu
vinegar	酢、ビネガー	su, binegā

anise	アニス	anisu
basil	バジル	bajiru
cloves	クローブ	kurōbu
ginger	生姜、ジンジャー	shōga, jinjā
coriander	コリアンダー	koriandā
cinnamon	シナモン	shinamon

sesame	ゴマ［胡麻］	goma
bay leaf	ローリエ	rōrie
paprika	パプリカ	papurika
caraway	キャラウェイ	kyarawei
saffron	サフラン	safuran

42. Meals

food	食べ物	tabemono
to eat (vi, vt)	食べる	taberu
breakfast	朝食	chōshoku
to have breakfast	朝食をとる	chōshoku wo toru
lunch	昼食	chūshoku
to have lunch	昼食をとる	chūshoku wo toru
dinner	夕食	yūshoku
to have dinner	夕食をとる	yūshoku wo toru
appetite	食欲	shokuyoku
Enjoy your meal!	どうぞお召し上がり下さい！	dōzo o meshiagarikudasai!

to open (~ a bottle)	開ける	akeru
to spill (liquid)	こぼす	kobosu
to spill out (vi)	こぼれる	koboreru
to boil (vi)	沸く	waku
to boil (vt)	沸かす	wakasu
boiled (~ water)	沸騰させた	futtō sase ta
to chill, cool down (vt)	冷やす	hiyasu
to chill (vi)	冷える	hieru
taste, flavor	味	aji
aftertaste	後味	atoaji
to be on a diet	ダイエットをする	daietto wo suru
diet	ダイエット	daietto
vitamin	ビタミン	bitamin
calorie	カロリー	karorī
vegetarian (n)	ベジタリアン	bejitarian
vegetarian (adj)	ベジタリアン用の	bejitarian yōno
fats (nutrient)	脂肪	shibō
proteins	タンパク質 [蛋白質]	tanpaku shitsu
carbohydrates	炭水化物	tansuikabutsu
slice (of lemon, ham)	スライス	suraisu
piece (of cake, pie)	一切れ	ichi kire
crumb (of bread)	くず	kuzu

43. Table setting

spoon	スプーン	supūn
knife	ナイフ	naifu
fork	フォーク	fōku
cup (of coffee)	カップ	kappu
plate (dinner ~)	皿	sara
saucer	ソーサー	sōsā
napkin (on table)	ナフキン	nafukin
toothpick	つまようじ [爪楊枝]	tsumayōji

44. Restaurant

restaurant	レストラン	resutoran
coffee house	喫茶店	kissaten
pub, bar	パブ、バー	pabu, bā
tearoom	喫茶店	kissaten
waiter	ウェイター	weitā
waitress	ウェートレス	wētoresu

bartender	バーテンダー	bātendā
menu	メニュー	menyū
wine list	ワインリスト	wain risuto
to book a table	テーブルを予約する	tēburu wo yoyaku suru
course, dish	料理	ryōri
to order (meal)	注文する	chūmon suru
to make an order	注文する	chūmon suru
aperitif	アペリティフ	aperitifu
appetizer	前菜	zensai
dessert	デザート	dezāto
check	お勘定	okanjō
to pay the check	勘定を払う	kanjō wo harau
to give change	釣り銭を渡す	tsurisen wo watasu
tip	チップ	chippu

Family, relatives and friends

45. Personal information. Forms

name, first name	名前	namae
family name	姓	sei
date of birth	誕生日	tanjō bi
place of birth	出生地	shusseichi
nationality	国籍	kokuseki
place of residence	住所	jūsho
country	国	kuni
profession (occupation)	職業	shokugyō
gender, sex	性	sei
height	身長	shinchō
weight	体重	taijū

46. Family members. Relatives

mother	母親	hahaoya
father	父親	chichioya
son	息子	musuko
daughter	娘	musume
younger daughter	下の娘	shitano musume
younger son	下の息子	shitano musuko
eldest daughter	長女	chōjo
eldest son	長男	chōnan
brother	兄、弟、兄弟	ani, otōto, kyoōdai
elder brother	兄	ani
younger brother	弟	otōto
sister	姉、妹、姉妹	ane, imōto, shimai
elder sister	姉	ane
younger sister	妹	imōto
cousin (masc.)	従兄弟	itoko
cousin (fem.)	従姉妹	itoko
mom	お母さん	okāsan
dad, daddy	お父さん	otōsan
parents	親	oya
child	子供	kodomo
children	子供	kodomo

grandmother	祖母	sobo
grandfather	祖父	sofu
grandson	孫息子	mago musuko
granddaughter	孫娘	mago musume
grandchildren	孫	mago
uncle	伯父	oji
aunt	伯母	oba
nephew	甥	oi
niece	姪	mei
mother-in-law (wife's mother)	妻の母親	tsuma no hahaoya
father-in-law (husband's father)	義父	gifu
son-in-law (daughter's husband)	娘の夫	musume no otto
stepmother	継母	keibo
stepfather	継父	keifu
infant	乳児	nyūji
baby (infant)	赤ん坊	akanbō
little boy, kid	子供	kodomo
wife	妻	tsuma
husband	夫	otto
spouse (husband)	配偶者	haigū sha
spouse (wife)	配偶者	haigū sha
married (masc.)	既婚の	kikon no
married (fem.)	既婚の	kikon no
single (unmarried)	独身の	dokushin no
bachelor	独身男性	dokushin dansei
divorced (masc.)	離婚した	rikon shi ta
widow	未亡人	mibōjin
widower	男やもめ	otokoyamome
relative	親戚	shinseki
close relative	近い親戚	chikai shinseki
distant relative	遠い親戚	tōi shinseki
relatives	親族	shinzoku
orphan (boy or girl)	孤児	koji
guardian (of minor)	後見人	kōkennin
to adopt (a boy)	養子にする	yōshi ni suru
to adopt (a girl)	養女にする	yōjo ni suru

Medicine

47. Diseases

sickness	病気	byōki
to be sick	病気になる	byōki ni naru
health	健康	kenkō
runny nose (coryza)	鼻水	hanamizu
angina	狭心症	kyōshinshō
cold (illness)	風邪	kaze
to catch a cold	風邪をひく	kaze wo hiku
bronchitis	気管支炎	kikanshien
pneumonia	肺炎	haien
flu, influenza	インフルエンザ	infuruenza
near-sighted (adj)	近視の	kinshi no
far-sighted (adj)	遠視の	enshi no
strabismus (crossed eyes)	斜視	shashi
cross-eyed (adj)	斜視の	shashi no
cataract	白内障	hakunaishō
glaucoma	緑内障	ryokunaishō
stroke	脳卒中	nōsocchū
heart attack	心臓発作	shinzō hossa
myocardial infarction	心筋梗塞	shinkinkōsoku
paralysis	まひ ［麻痺］	mahi
to paralyze (vt)	まひさせる	mahi saseru
allergy	アレルギー	arerugī
asthma	ぜんそく ［喘息］	zensoku
diabetes	糖尿病	tōnyō byō
toothache	歯痛	shitsū
caries	カリエス	kariesu
diarrhea	下痢	geri
constipation	便秘	benpi
stomach upset	胃のむかつき	i no mukatsuki
food poisoning	食中毒	shokuchūdoku
to have a food poisoning	食中毒にかかる	shokuchūdoku ni kakaru
arthritis	関節炎	kansetsu en
rickets	くる病	kuru yamai
rheumatism	リューマチ	ryūmachi

atherosclerosis	アテローム性動脈硬化	ate rōmu sei dōmyaku kōka
gastritis	胃炎	ien
appendicitis	虫垂炎	chūsuien
cholecystitis	胆嚢炎	tannō en
ulcer	潰瘍	kaiyō
measles	麻疹	hashika
German measles	風疹	fūshin
jaundice	黄疸	ōdan
hepatitis	肝炎	kanen
schizophrenia	統合失調症	tōgō shicchō shō
rabies (hydrophobia)	恐水病	kyōsuibyō
neurosis	神経症	shinkeishō
concussion	脳震とう（脳震盪）	nōshintō
cancer	がん［癌］	gan
sclerosis	硬化症	kōka shō
multiple sclerosis	多発性硬化症	tahatsu sei kōka shō
alcoholism	アルコール依存症	arukōru izon shō
alcoholic (n)	アルコール依存症患者	arukōru izon shō kanja
syphilis	梅毒	baidoku
AIDS	エイズ	eizu
tumor	腫瘍	shuyō
malignant (adj)	悪性の	akusei no
benign (adj)	良性の	ryōsei no
fever	発熱	hatsunetsu
malaria	マラリア	mararia
gangrene	壊疽	eso
seasickness	船酔い	fune yoi
epilepsy	てんかん［癲癇］	tenkan
epidemic	伝染病	densen byō
typhus	チフス	chifusu
tuberculosis	結核	kekkaku
cholera	コレラ	korera
plague (bubonic ~)	ペスト	pesuto

48. Symptoms. Treatments. Part 1

symptom	兆候	chōkō
temperature	体温	taion
high temperature	熱	netsu
pulse	脈拍	myakuhaku
giddiness	目まい［眩暈］	memai
hot (adj)	熱い	atsui

shivering	震え	furue
pale (e.g., ~ face)	青白い	aojiroi
cough	咳	seki
to cough (vi)	咳をする	seki wo suru
to sneeze (vi)	くしゃみをする	kushami wo suru
faint	気絶	kizetsu
to faint (vi)	気絶する	kizetsu suru
bruise (hématome)	打ち身	uchimi
bump (lump)	たんこぶ	tankobu
to bruise oneself	あざができる	aza ga dekiru
bruise (contusion)	打撲傷	dabokushō
to get bruised	打撲する	daboku suru
to limp (vi)	足を引きずる	ashi wo hikizuru
dislocation	脱臼	dakkyū
to dislocate (vt)	脱臼する	dakkyū suru
fracture	骨折	kossetsu
to have a fracture	骨折する	kossetsu suru
cut (e.g., paper ~)	切り傷	kirikizu
to cut oneself	切り傷を負う	kirikizu wo ō
bleeding	出血	shukketsu
burn (injury)	火傷	yakedo
to scald oneself	火傷する	yakedo suru
to prick (vt)	刺す	sasu
to prick oneself	自分を刺す	jibun wo sasu
to injure (vt)	けがする	kega suru
injury	けが [怪我]	kega
wound	負傷	fushō
trauma	外傷	gaishō
to be delirious	熱に浮かされる	netsu ni ukasareru
to stutter (vi)	どもる	domoru
sunstroke	日射病	nisshabyō

49. Symptoms. Treatments. Part 2

pain	痛み	itami
splinter (in foot, etc.)	とげ [棘]	toge
sweat (perspiration)	汗	ase
to sweat (perspire)	汗をかく	ase wo kaku
vomiting	嘔吐	ōto
convulsions	けいれん [痙攣]	keiren
pregnant (adj)	妊娠している	ninshin shi te iru
to be born	生まれる	umareru

delivery, labor	分娩	bumben
to deliver (~ a baby)	分娩する	bumben suru
abortion	妊娠中絶	ninshin chūzetsu
breathing, respiration	呼吸	kokyū
inhalation	息を吸うこと	iki wo sū koto
exhalation	息を吐くこと	iki wo haku koto
to exhale (vi)	息を吐く	iki wo haku
to inhale (vi)	息を吸う	iki wo sū
disabled person	障害者	shōgai sha
cripple	身障者	shinshōsha
drug addict	麻薬中毒者	mayaku chūdoku sha
deaf (adj)	ろうの [聾の]	rō no
dumb, mute	口のきけない	kuchi no kike nai
deaf-and-dumb (adj)	ろうあの [聾唖の]	rōa no
mad, insane (adj)	狂気の	kyōki no
madman	狂人	kyōjin
madwoman	狂女	kyōjo
to go insane	気が狂う	ki ga kurū
gene	遺伝子	idenshi
immunity	免疫	meneki
hereditary (adj)	遺伝性の	iden sei no
congenital (adj)	先天性の	senten sei no
virus	ウィルス	wirusu
microbe	細菌	saikin
bacterium	バクテリア	bakuteria
infection	伝染	densen

50. Symptoms. Treatments. Part 3

hospital	病院	byōin
patient	患者	kanja
diagnosis	診断	shindan
cure	療養	ryōyō
medical treatment	治療	chiryō
to get treatment	治療を受ける	chiryō wo ukeru
to treat (vt)	治療する	chiryō suru
to nurse (look after)	看護する	kango suru
care (nursing ~)	看護	kango
operation, surgery	手術	shujutsu
to bandage (head, limb)	包帯をする	hōtai wo suru
bandaging	包帯を巻くこと	hōtai wo maku koto
vaccination	予防接種	yobō sesshu

to vaccinate (vt)	予防接種をする	yobō sesshu wo suru
injection, shot	注射	chūsha
to give an injection	注射する	chūsha suru
attack	発作	hossa
amputation	切断手術	setsudan shujutsu
to amputate (vt)	切断する	setsudan suru
coma	昏睡	konsui
to be in a coma	昏睡状態になる	konsui jōtai ni naru
intensive care	集中治療	shūchū chiryō
to recover (~ from flu)	回復する	kaifuku suru
state (patient's ~)	体調	taichō
consciousness	意識	ishiki
memory (faculty)	記憶	kioku
to extract (tooth)	抜く	nuku
filling	詰め物	tsume mono
to fill (a tooth)	詰め物をする	tsume mono wo suru
hypnosis	催眠術	saimin jutsu
to hypnotize (vt)	催眠術をかける	saimin jutsu wo kakeru

51. Doctors

doctor	医者	isha
nurse	看護師	kangoshi
private physician	町医者	machīsha
dentist	歯科医	shikai
ophthalmologist	眼科医	gankai
internist	内科医	naikai
surgeon	外科医	gekai
psychiatrist	精神科医	seishin kai
pediatrician	小児科医	shōnikai
psychologist	心理学者	shinri gakusha
gynecologist	婦人科医	fujin kai
cardiologist	心臓内科医	shinzō naikai

52. Medicine. Drugs. Accessories

medicine, drug	薬	kusuri
remedy	治療薬	chiryō yaku
to prescribe (vt)	処方する	shohō suru
prescription	処方	shohō
tablet, pill	錠剤	jōzai
ointment	軟膏	nankō

ampule	アンプル	anpuru
mixture	調合薬	chōgō yaku
syrup	シロップ	shiroppu
pill	丸剤	gan zai
powder	粉薬	konagusuri
bandage	包帯	hōtai
cotton wool	脱脂綿	dasshimen
iodine	ヨード	yōdo
Band-Aid	ばんそうこう［絆創膏］	bansōkō
eyedropper	アイドロッパー	aidoroppā
thermometer	体温計	taionkei
syringe	注射器	chūsha ki
wheelchair	車椅子	kurumaisu
crutches	松葉杖	matsubazue
painkiller	痛み止め	itami tome
laxative	下剤	gezai
spirit (ethanol)	エタノール	etanoru
medicinal herbs	薬草	yakusō
herbal (~ tea)	薬草の	yakusō no

HUMAN HABITAT

City

53. City. Life in the city

city, town	市、町	shi, machi
capital city	首都	shuto
village	村	mura
city map	市街地図	shigai chizu
downtown	中心街	chūshin gai
suburb	郊外	kōgai
suburban (adj)	郊外の	kōgai no
outskirts	町外れ	machihazure
environs (suburbs)	近郊	kinkō
city block	街区	gaiku
residential block	住宅街	jūtaku gai
traffic	交通	kōtsū
traffic lights	信号	shingō
public transportation	公共交通機関	kōkyō kōtsū kikan
intersection	交差点	kōsaten
crosswalk	横断歩道	ōdan hodō
pedestrian underpass	地下道	chikadō
to cross (vt)	横断する	ōdan suru
pedestrian	歩行者	hokō sha
sidewalk	歩道	hodō
bridge	橋	hashi
bank (riverbank)	堤防	teibō
fountain	噴水	funsui
allée	散歩道	sanpomichi
park	公園	kōen
boulevard	大通り	ōdōri
square	広場	hiroba
avenue (wide street)	アヴェニュー	avenyū
street	通り	tōri
side street	わき道 [脇道]	wakimichi
dead end	行き止まり	ikidomari
house	家屋	kaoku
building	建物	tatemono

skyscraper	摩天楼	matenrō
facade	ファサード	fasādo
roof	屋根	yane
window	窓	mado
arch	アーチ	āchi
column	柱	hashira
corner	角	kado
store window	ショーウインドー	shōuindō
store sign	店看板	mise kanban
poster	ポスター	posutā
advertising poster	広告ポスター	kōkoku posutā
billboard	広告掲示板	kōkoku keijiban
garbage, trash	ゴミ［ごみ］	gomi
garbage can	ゴミ入れ	gomi ire
to litter (vi)	ゴミを投げ捨てる	gomi wo nagesuteru
garbage dump	ゴミ捨て場	gomi suteba
phone booth	電話ボックス	denwa bokkusu
lamppost	街灯柱	gaitō bashira
bench (park ~)	ベンチ	benchi
police officer	警官	keikan
police	警察	keisatsu
beggar	こじき	kojiki
homeless, bum	ホームレス	hōmuresu

54. Urban institutions

store	店、…屋	mise, …ya
drugstore, pharmacy	薬局	yakkyoku
optical store	眼鏡店	megane ten
shopping mall	ショッピングモール	shoppingu mōru
supermarket	スーパーマーケット	sūpāmāketto
bakery	パン屋	panya
baker	パン職人	pan shokunin
candy store	菓子店	kashi ten
grocery store	食料品店	shokuryō hin ten
butcher shop	肉屋	nikuya
produce store	八百屋	yaoya
market	市場	ichiba
coffee house	喫茶店	kissaten
restaurant	レストラン	resutoran
pub	パブ	pabu
pizzeria	ピザ屋	piza ya
hair salon	美容院	biyō in

post office	郵便局	yūbin kyoku
dry cleaners	クリーニング屋	kurīningu ya
photo studio	写真館	shashin kan
shoe store	靴屋	kutsuya
bookstore	本屋	honya
sporting goods store	スポーツ店	supōtsu ten
clothes repair	洋服直し専門店	yōfuku naoshi senmon ten
formal wear rental	貸衣裳店	kashi ishō ten
movie rental store	レンタルビデオ店	rentarubideo ten
circus	サーカス	sākasu
zoo	動物園	dōbutsu en
movie theater	映画館	eiga kan
museum	博物館	hakubutsukan
library	図書館	toshokan
theater	劇場	gekijō
opera	オペラハウス	opera hausu
nightclub	ナイトクラブ	naito kurabu
casino	カジノ	kajino
mosque	モスク	mosuku
synagogue	シナゴーグ	shinagōgu
cathedral	大聖堂	dai seidō
temple	寺院	jīn
church	教会	kyōkai
college	大学	daigaku
university	大学	daigaku
school	学校	gakkō
prefecture	県庁舎	ken chōsha
city hall	市役所	shiyaku sho
hotel	ホテル	hoteru
bank	銀行	ginkō
embassy	大使館	taishikan
travel agency	旅行代理店	ryokō dairi ten
information office	案内所	annai sho
money exchange	両替所	ryōgae sho
subway	地下鉄	chikatetsu
hospital	病院	byōin
gas station	ガソリンスタンド	gasorin sutando
parking lot	駐車場	chūsha jō

55. Signs

store sign	店看板	mise kanban
notice (written text)	看板	kanban
poster	ポスター	posutā
direction sign	方向看板	hōkō kanban
arrow (sign)	矢印	yajirushi
caution	注意	chūi
warning sign	警告表示	keikoku hyōji
to warn (vt)	警告する	keikoku suru
day off	定休日	teikyū bi
timetable (schedule)	営業時間の看板	eigyō jikan no kanban
opening hours	営業時間	eigyō jikan
WELCOME!	ようこそ	yōkoso
ENTRANCE	入口	iriguchi
EXIT	出口	deguchi
PUSH	押す	osu
PULL	引く	hiku
OPEN	営業中	eigyō chū
CLOSED	休業日	kyūgyōbi
WOMEN	女性	josei
MEN	男性	dansei
DISCOUNTS	割引	waribiki
SALE	バーゲンセール	bāgen sēru
NEW!	新発売！	shin hatsubai!
FREE	無料	muryō
ATTENTION!	ご注意！	go chūi!
NO VACANCIES	満室	manshitsu
RESERVED	御予約席	go yoyaku seki
ADMINISTRATION	支配人	shihainin
STAFF ONLY	関係者以外立入禁止	kankei sha igai tachīrikinshi
BEWARE OF THE DOG!	猛犬注意	mōken chūi
NO SMOKING	禁煙	kinen
DO NOT TOUCH!	手を触れるな	te wo fureru na
DANGEROUS	危険	kiken
DANGER	危険	kiken
HIGH TENSION	高電圧	kō denatsu
NO SWIMMING!	水泳禁止	suiei kinshi
OUT OF ORDER	故障中	koshō chū
FLAMMABLE	可燃性物質	kanen sei busshitsu

FORBIDDEN	禁止	kinshi
NO TRESPASSING!	通り抜け禁止	tōrinuke kinshi
WET PAINT	ペンキ塗りたて	penki nuritate

56. Urban transportation

bus	バス	basu
streetcar	路面電車	romen densha
trolley	トロリーバス	tororībasu
route (of bus)	路線	rosen
number (e.g., bus ~)	番号	bangō

to go by ...	…で行く	… de iku
to get on (~ the bus)	乗る	noru
to get off ...	降りる	oriru

stop (e.g., bus ~)	停	toma
next stop	次の停車駅	tsugi no teishaeki
terminus	終着駅	shūchakueki
schedule	時刻表	jikoku hyō
to wait (vt)	待つ	matsu

| ticket | 乗車券 | jōsha ken |
| fare | 運賃 | unchin |

cashier (ticket seller)	販売員	hanbai in
ticket inspection	集札	shū satsu
conductor	車掌	shashō

to be late (for ...)	遅れる	okureru
to miss (~ the train, etc.)	逃す	nogasu
to be in a hurry	急ぐ	isogu

taxi, cab	タクシー	takushī
taxi driver	タクシーの運転手	takushī no unten shu
by taxi	タクシーで	takushī de
taxi stand	タクシー乗り場	takushī noriba
to call a taxi	タクシーを呼ぶ	takushī wo yobu
to take a taxi	タクシーに乗る	takushī ni noru

traffic	交通	kōtsū
traffic jam	渋滞	jūtai
rush hour	ラッシュアワー	rasshuawā
to park (vi)	駐車する	chūsha suru
to park (vt)	駐車する	chūsha suru
parking lot	駐車場	chūsha jō

subway	地下鉄	chikatetsu
station	駅	eki
to take the subway	地下鉄で行く	chikatetsu de iku

| train | 列車 | ressha |
| train station | 鉄道駅 | tetsudō eki |

57. Sightseeing

monument	記念碑	kinen hi
fortress	要塞	yōsai
palace	宮殿	kyūden
castle	城	shiro
tower	塔	tō
mausoleum	マウソレウム	mausoreumu

architecture	建築	kenchiku
medieval (adj)	中世の	chūsei no
ancient (adj)	古代の	kodai no
national (adj)	国の	kuni no
well-known (adj)	有名な	yūmei na

tourist	観光客	kankō kyaku
guide (person)	ガイド	gaido
excursion, guided tour	小旅行	shō ryokō
to show (vt)	案内する	annai suru
to tell (vt)	話をする	hanashi wo suru

to find (vt)	見つける	mitsukeru
to get lost (lose one's way)	道に迷う	michi ni mayō
map (e.g., subway ~)	地図	chizu
map (e.g., city ~)	地図	chizu

souvenir, gift	土産	miyage
gift shop	土産品店	miyage hin ten
to take pictures	写真に撮る	shashin ni toru
to be photographed	写真を撮られる	shashin wo torareru

58. Shopping

to buy (purchase)	買う	kau
purchase	買い物	kaimono
to go shopping	買い物に行く	kaimono ni iku
shopping	ショッピング	shoppingu

| to be open (ab. store) | 開いている | hiraite iru |
| to be closed | 閉まっている | shimatte iru |

footwear	履物	hakimono
clothes, clothing	洋服	yōfuku
cosmetics	化粧品	keshō hin
food products	食料品	shokuryō hin

gift, present	土産	miyage
salesman	店員、売り子	tenin, uriko
saleswoman	店員、売り子	tenin, uriko
check out, cash desk	レジ	reji
mirror	鏡	kagami
counter (in shop)	カウンター	kauntā
fitting room	試着室	shichaku shitsu
to try on	試着する	shichaku suru
to fit (ab. dress, etc.)	合う	au
to like (I like ...)	好む	konomu
price	価格	kakaku
price tag	値札	nefuda
to cost (vt)	かかる	kakaru
How much?	いくら？	ikura ?
discount	割引	waribiki
inexpensive (adj)	安価な	anka na
cheap (adj)	安い	yasui
expensive (adj)	高い	takai
It's expensive	それは高い	sore wa takai
rental (n)	レンタル	rentaru
to rent (~ a tuxedo)	レンタルする	rentaru suru
credit	信用取引	shinyō torihiki
on credit (adv)	付けで	tsuke de

59. Money

money	お金	okane
currency exchange	両替	ryōgae
exchange rate	為替レート	kawase rēto
ATM	ATM	ētīemu
coin	コイン	koin
dollar	ドル	doru
euro	ユーロ	yūro
lira	リラ	rira
Deutschmark	ドイツマルク	doitsu maruku
franc	フラン	furan
pound sterling	スターリング・ポンド	sutāringu pondo
yen	円	en
debt	債務	saimu
debtor	債務者	saimu sha
to lend (money)	貸す	kasu
to borrow (vi, vt)	借りる	kariru

bank	銀行	ginkō
account	口座	kōza
to deposit (vt)	預金する	yokin suru
to deposit into the account	口座に預金する	kōza ni yokin suru
to withdraw (vt)	引き出す	hikidasu

credit card	クレジットカード	kurejitto kādo
cash	現金	genkin
check	小切手	kogitte
to write a check	小切手を書く	kogitte wo kaku
checkbook	小切手帳	kogitte chō

wallet	財布	saifu
change purse	小銭入れ	kozeni ire
billfold	札入れ	satsu ire
safe	金庫	kinko

heir	相続人	sōzokunin
inheritance	相続	sōzoku
fortune (wealth)	財産	zaisan

lease, rent	賃貸	chintai
rent money	家賃	yachin
to rent (sth from sb)	借りる	kariru

price	価格	kakaku
cost	費用	hiyō
sum	合計金額	gōkei kingaku

to spend (vt)	お金を使う	okane wo tsukau
expenses	出費	shuppi
to economize (vi, vt)	倹約する	kenyaku suru
economical	節約の	setsuyaku no

to pay (vi, vt)	払う	harau
payment	支払い	shiharai
change (give the ~)	おつり	o tsuri

tax	税	zei
fine	罰金	bakkin
to fine (vt)	罰金を科す	bakkin wo kasu

60. Post. Postal service

post office	郵便局	yūbin kyoku
mail (letters, etc.)	郵便物	yūbin butsu
mailman	郵便配達人	yūbin haitatsu jin
opening hours	営業時間	eigyō jikan
letter	手紙	tegami
registered letter	書留郵便	kakitome yūbin

postcard	はがき [葉書]	hagaki
telegram	電報	denpō
parcel	小包	kozutsumi
money transfer	送金	sōkin
to receive (vt)	受け取る	uketoru
to send (vt)	送る	okuru
sending	送信	sōshin
address	住所	jūsho
ZIP code	郵便番号	yūbin bangō
sender	送り主	okurinushi
receiver, addressee	受取人	uketorinin
name	名前	namae
family name	姓	sei
rate (of postage)	郵便料金	yūbin ryōkin
standard (adj)	通常の	tsūjō no
economical (adj)	エコノミー航空	ekonomīkōkū
weight	重さ	omo sa
to weigh up (vt)	量る	hakaru
envelope	封筒	fūtō
postage stamp	郵便切手	yūbin kitte
to stamp an envelope	封筒に切手を貼る	fūtō ni kitte wo haru

Dwelling. House. Home

61. House. Electricity

electricity	電気	denki
light bulb	電球	denkyū
switch	スイッチ	suicchi
fuse	ヒューズ	hyūzu
cable, wire (electric ~)	電線、ケーブル	densen, kēburu
wiring	電気配線	denki haisen
electricity meter	電気メーター	denki mētā
readings	検針値	kenshin chi

62. Villa. Mansion

country house	田舎の邸宅	inaka no teitaku
villa (by sea)	別荘	bessō
wing (of building)	翼棟	yokutō
garden	庭	niwa
park	庭園	teien
tropical greenhouse	温室	onshitsu
to look after (garden, etc.)	手入れをする	teire wo suru
swimming pool	プール	pūru
gym	ジム	jimu
tennis court	テニスコート	tenisu kōto
home theater room	ホームシアター	hōmu shiatā
garage	車庫	shako
private property	私有地	shiyūchi
private land	民有地	minyū chi
warning (caution)	警告	keikoku
warning sign	警告表示	keikoku hyōji
security	警備	keibi
security guard	警備員	keibi in
burglar alarm	強盗警報機	gōtō keihō ki

63. Apartment

apartment	アパート	apāto
room	部屋	heya
bedroom	寝室	shinshitsu
dining room	食堂	shokudō
living room	居間	ima
study (home office)	書斎	shosai
entry room	玄関	genkan
bathroom	浴室	yokushitsu
half bath	トイレ	toire
ceiling	天井	tenjō
floor	床	yuka
corner	隅	sumi

64. Furniture. Interior

furniture	家具	kagu
table	テーブル	tēburu
chair	椅子	isu
bed	ベッド	beddo
couch, sofa	ソファ	sofa
armchair	肘掛け椅子	hijikake isu
bookcase	書棚	shodana
shelf	棚	tana
set of shelves	違い棚	chigaidana
wardrobe	ワードローブ	wādo rōbu
coat rack	ウォールハンガー	wōru hangā
coat stand	コートスタンド	kōto sutando
dresser	チェスト	chesuto
coffee table	コーヒーテーブル	kōhī tēburu
mirror	鏡	kagami
carpet	カーペット	kāpetto
rug, small carpet	マット	matto
fireplace	暖炉	danro
candle	ろうそく	rōsoku
candlestick	ろうそく立て	rōsoku date
drapes	カーテン	kāten
wallpaper	壁紙	kabegami
blinds (jalousie)	ブラインド	buraindo
table lamp	テーブルランプ	tēburu ranpu

wall lamp (sconce)	ウォールランプ	wōru ranpu
floor lamp	フロアスタンド	furoa sutando
chandelier	シャンデリア	shanderia
leg (of chair, table)	脚	ashi
armrest	肘掛け	hijikake
back (backrest)	背もたれ	semotare
drawer	引き出し	hikidashi

65. Bedding

bedclothes	寝具	shingu
pillow	枕	makura
pillowcase	枕カバー	makura kabā
blanket (comforter)	毛布	mōfu
sheet	シーツ	shītsu
bedspread	ベッドカバー	beddo kabā

66. Kitchen

kitchen	台所	daidokoro
gas	ガス	gasu
gas cooker	ガスコンロ	gasu konro
electric cooker	電気コンロ	denki konro
oven	オーブン	ōbun
microwave oven	電子レンジ	denshi renji
refrigerator	冷蔵庫	reizōko
freezer	冷凍庫	reitōko
dishwasher	食器洗い機	shokkiarai ki
meat grinder	肉挽き器	niku hiki ki
juicer	ジューサー	jūsā
toaster	トースター	tōsutā
mixer	ハンドミキサー	hando mikisā
coffee maker	コーヒーメーカー	kōhī mēkā
coffee pot	コーヒーポット	kōhī potto
coffee grinder	コーヒーグラインダー	kōhī guraindā
kettle	やかん	yakan
teapot	急須	kyūsu
lid	蓋 [ふた]	futa
tea strainer	茶漉し	chakoshi
spoon	さじ [匙]	saji
teaspoon	茶さじ	cha saji
tablespoon	大さじ [大匙]	ōsaji

| fork | フォーク | fōku |
| knife | ナイフ | naifu |

tableware (dishes)	食器	shokki
plate (dinner ~)	皿	sara
saucer	ソーサー	sōsā

shot glass	ショットグラス	shotto gurasu
glass (~ of water)	コップ	koppu
cup	カップ	kappu

sugar bowl	砂糖入れ	satō ire
salt shaker	塩入れ	shio ire
pepper shaker	胡椒入れ	koshō ire
butter dish	バター皿	batā zara

saucepan	両手鍋	ryō tenabe
frying pan	フライパン	furaipan
ladle	おたま	o tama
colander	水切りボール	mizukiri bōru
tray	配膳盆	haizen bon

bottle	ボトル	botoru
jar (glass)	ジャー、瓶	jā, bin
can	缶	kan

bottle opener	栓抜き	sen nuki
can opener	缶切り	kankiri
corkscrew	コルク抜き	koruku nuki
filter	フィルター	firutā
to filter (vt)	フィルターにかける	firutā ni kakeru

| trash | ゴミ［ごみ］ | gomi |
| trash can | ゴミ箱 | gomibako |

67. Bathroom

bathroom	浴室	yokushitsu
water	水	mizu
tap, faucet	蛇口	jaguchi
hot water	温水	onsui
cold water	冷水	reisui

toothpaste	歯磨き粉	hamigakiko
to brush one's teeth	歯を磨く	ha wo migaku
toothbrush	歯ブラシ	haburashi

to shave (vi)	ひげを剃る	hige wo soru
shaving foam	シェービングフォーム	shēbingu fōmu
razor	剃刀	kamisori

to wash (one's hands, etc.)	洗う	arau
to take a bath	風呂に入る	furo ni hairu
shower	シャワー	shawā
to take a shower	シャワーを浴びる	shawā wo abiru
bathtub	浴槽	yokusō
toilet (toilet bowl)	トイレ、便器	toire, benki
sink (washbasin)	洗面台	senmen dai
soap	石鹸	sekken
soap dish	石鹸皿	sekken zara
sponge	スポンジ	suponji
shampoo	シャンプー	shanpū
towel	タオル	taoru
bathrobe	バスローブ	basurōbu
laundry (process)	洗濯	sentaku
washing machine	洗濯機	sentaku ki
to do the laundry	洗濯する	sentaku suru
laundry detergent	洗剤	senzai

68. Household appliances

TV set	テレビ	terebi
tape recorder	テープレコーダー	tēpurekōdā
video, VCR	ビデオ	bideo
radio	ラジオ	rajio
player (CD, MP3, etc.)	プレーヤー	purēyā
video projector	ビデオプロジェクター	bideo purojekutā
home movie theater	ホームシアター	hōmu shiatā
DVD player	DVDプレーヤー	dībuidī purēyā
amplifier	アンプ	anpu
video game console	ゲーム機	gēmu ki
video camera	ビデオカメラ	bideo kamera
camera (photo)	カメラ	kamera
digital camera	デジタルカメラ	dejitaru kamera
vacuum cleaner	掃除機	sōji ki
iron (e.g., steam ~)	アイロン	airon
ironing board	アイロン台	airondai
telephone	電話	denwa
mobile phone	携帯電話	keitai denwa
typewriter	タイプライター	taipuraitā
sewing machine	ミシン	mishin
microphone	マイクロフォン	maikurofon
headphones	ヘッドホン	heddohon

remote control (TV)	リモコン	rimokon
CD, compact disc	CD（シーディー）	shīdī
cassette	カセットテープ	kasettotēpu
vinyl record	レコード	rekōdo

HUMAN ACTIVITIES

Job. Business. Part 1

69. Office. Working in the office

office (of firm)	オフィス	ofisu
office (of director, etc.)	室	shitsu
front desk	受付	uketsuke
secretary	秘書	hisho
secretary (fem.)	秘書	hisho
director	責任者	sekinin sha
manager	マネージャー	manējā
accountant	会計士	kaikeishi
employee	社員	shain
furniture	家具	kagu
desk	デスク	desuku
desk chair	ワーキングチェア	wākingu chea
chest of drawers	キャビネット	kyabinetto
coat stand	コートスタンド	kōto sutando
computer	コンピューター	konpyūtā
printer	プリンター	purintā
fax machine	ファックス	fakkusu
photocopier	コピー機	kopī ki
paper	用紙	yōshi
office supplies	事務用品	jimu yōhin
mouse pad	マウスパッド	mausu paddo
sheet (of paper)	一枚の紙	ichimai no kami
folder, binder	バインダー	baindā
catalog	カタログ	katarogu
phone book (directory)	電話帳	denwa chō
documentation	付随資料	fuzui shiryō
brochure (e.g., 12 pages ~)	パンフレット	panfuretto
leaflet	チラシ	chirashi
sample	見本	mihon
training meeting	研修	kenshū
meeting (of managers)	会議	kaigi
lunch time	昼食時間	chūshoku jikan

to make a copy	コピーする	kopī suru
to make copies	複数部コピーする	fukusū bu kopī suru
to receive a fax	ファックスを受け取る	fakkusu wo uketoru
to send a fax	ファクスを送る	fakusu wo okuru
to call (by phone)	電話する	denwa suru
to answer (vt)	出る	deru
to put through	電話をつなぐ	denwa wo tsunagu
to arrange, to set up	段取りをつける	dandori wo tsukeru
to demonstrate (vt)	デモをする	demo wo suru
to be absent	欠席する	kesseki suru
absence	欠席	kesseki

70. Business processes. Part 1

business	商売	shōbai
occupation	職業	shokugyō
firm	会社	kaisha
company	会社	kaisha
corporation	法人	hōjin
enterprise	企業	kigyō
agency	代理店	dairi ten
agreement (contract)	合意書	gōi sho
contract	契約	keiyaku
deal	取引	torihiki
order (to place an ~)	注文	chūmon
term (of contract)	条件	jōken
wholesale (adv)	卸売で	oroshiuri de
wholesale (adj)	卸売の	oroshiuri no
wholesale (n)	卸売り	oroshiuri
retail (adj)	小売の	kōri no
retail (n)	小売り	kōri
competitor	競争相手	kyōsō aite
competition	競争	kyōsō
to compete (vi)	競争する	kyōsō suru
partner (associate)	パートナー	pātonā
partnership	協力関係	kyōryoku kankei
crisis	危機	kiki
bankruptcy	破産	hasan
to go bankrupt	破産する	hasan suru
difficulty	困難	konnan
problem	問題	mondai
catastrophe	大失敗	dai shippai
economy	景気	keiki

economic (~ growth)	景気の	keiki no
economic recession	景気後退	keiki kōtai
goal (aim)	目標	mokuhyō
task	任務	ninmu
to trade (vi)	商売をする	shōbai wo suru
network (distribution ~)	網	mō
inventory (stock)	在庫	zaiko
assortment	仕分け	shiwake
leader (leading company)	トップ企業	toppu kigyō
large (~ company)	大手の	ōte no
monopoly	独占	dokusen
theory	理論	riron
practice	実務	jitsumu
experience (in my ~)	経験	keiken
trend (tendency)	傾向	keikō
development	発展	hatten

71. Business processes. Part 2

benefit, profit	利益	rieki
profitable (adj)	利益のある	rieki no aru
delegation (group)	代表団	daihyō dan
salary	給料	kyūryō
to correct (an error)	直す	naosu
business trip	出張	shucchō
commission	歩合	buai
to control (vt)	支配する	shihai suru
conference	会議	kaigi
license	免許	menkyo
reliable (~ partner)	信頼できる	shinrai dekiru
initiative (undertaking)	開始	kaishi
norm (standard)	標準	hyōjun
circumstance	状況	jōkyō
duty (of employee)	職務	shokumu
organization (company)	組織	soshiki
organization (process)	主催	shusai
organized (adj)	主催された	shusai sare ta
cancellation	取り消し	torikeshi
to cancel (call off)	取り消す	torikesu
report (official ~)	報告	hōkoku
patent	特許	tokkyo
to patent (obtain patent)	特許を取る	tokkyo wo toru

to plan (vt)	計画する	keikaku suru
bonus (money)	ボーナス	bōnasu
professional (adj)	専門的な	senmon teki na
procedure	手順	tejun

to examine (contract, etc.)	調べ上げる	shirabe ageru
calculation	計算	keisan
reputation	評判	hyōban
risk	リスク	risuku

to manage, to run	管理する	kanri suru
information	情報	jōhō
property	財産	zaisan
union	連合	rengō

life insurance	生命保険	seimei hoken
to insure (vt)	保険をかける	hoken wo kakeru
insurance	保険	hoken

auction (~ sale)	競売	kyōbai
to notify (inform)	通知する	tsūchi suru
management (process)	マネージメント	manējimento
service (~ industry)	サービス	sābisu

forum	公開討論会	kōkai tōron kai
to function (vi)	機能する	kinō suru
stage (phase)	段階	dankai
legal (~ services)	法律の	hōritsu no
lawyer (legal expert)	弁護士	bengoshi

72. Production. Works

plant	工場	kōba
factory	製造所	seizō sho
workshop	作業場	sagyōba
works, production site	生産現場	seisan genba

industry	産業	sangyō
industrial (adj)	産業の	sangyō no
heavy industry	重工業	jūkōgyō
light industry	軽工業	keikōgyō

products	生産物	seisan butsu
to produce (vt)	製造する	seisan suru
raw materials	原料	genryō

foreman	職長	shokuchō
workers team	作業チーム	sagyō chīmu
worker	作業員	sagyō in
working day	営業日	eigyōbi

pause	休憩 '	kyūkei
meeting	会議	kaigi
to discuss (vt)	討議する	tōgi suru

plan	計画	keikaku
to fulfill the plan	計画を実行する	keikaku wo jikkō suru
rate of output	生産率	seisan ritsu
quality	質	shitsu
checking (control)	検査	kensa
quality control	品質管理	hinshitsu kanri

work safety	労働安全	rōdō anzen
discipline	規律	kiritsu
violation	違反	ihan
(of safety rules, etc.)		
to violate (rules)	違反する	ihan suru

strike	ストライキ	sutoraiki
striker	ストライキをする人	sutoraiki wo suru hito
to be on strike	ストライキをする	sutoraiki wo suru
labor union	労働組合	rōdō kumiai

to invent (machine, etc.)	発明する	hatsumei suru
invention	発明	hatsumei
research	研究	kenkyū
to improve (make better)	改善する	kaizen suru

| technology | 技術 | gijutsu |
| technical drawing | 製図 | seizu |

load, cargo	積み荷	tsumini
loader (person)	荷役作業員	niyakusa gyōin
to load (vehicle, etc.)	積む	tsumu
loading (process)	荷役	niyaku

| to unload (vi, vt) | 下ろす | orosu |
| unloading | 荷下ろし [荷卸し] | ni oroshi |

transportation	輸送	yusō
transportation company	輸送会社	yusō gaisha
to transport (vt)	輸送する	yusō suru

freight car	貨車	kasha
cistern	タンク	tanku
truck	トラック	torakku

| machine tool | 工作機械 | kōsaku kikai |
| mechanism | 機械 | kikai |

industrial waste	産業廃棄物	sangyō haiki butsu
packing (process)	包装	hōsō
to pack (vt)	梱包する	konpō suru

73. Contract. Agreement

contract	契約	keiyaku
agreement	合意書	gōi sho
addendum	補遺	hoi
to sign a contract	契約書に署名する	keiyaku sho ni shomei suru
signature	署名	shomei
to sign (vt)	署名する	shomei suru
stamp (seal)	捺印	natsuin
subject of contract	契約の目的物	keiyaku no mokuteki butsu
clause	条項	jōkō
parties (in contract)	当事者	tōjisha
legal address	法的住所	hōteki jūsho
to break the contract	契約を破棄する	keiyaku wo haki suru
commitment	義務	gimu
responsibility	責任	sekinin
force majeure	不可抗力	fukakōryoku
dispute	係争	keisō
penalties	違約金	iyaku kin

74. Import & Export

import	輸入	yunyū
importer	輸入業者	yunyū gyōsha
to import (vt)	輸入する	yunyū suru
import (e.g., ~ goods)	輸入の	yunyū no
export	輸出	yushutsu
exporter	輸出業者	yushutsu gyōsha
to export (vi, vt)	輸出する	yushutsu suru
export (e.g., ~ goods)	輸出の	yushutsu no
goods	品物	shinamono
consignment, lot	委託	itaku
weight	重量	jūryō
volume	体積	taiseki
cubic meter	立法メートル	rippō mētoru
manufacturer	メーカー	mēkā
transportation company	輸送会社	yusō gaisha
container	コンテナ	kontena
border	国境	kokkyō
customs	税関	zeikan

customs duty	関税	kanzei
customs officer	税関吏	zeikanri
smuggling	密輸	mitsuyu
contraband (goods)	密輸された商品	mitsuyu sare ta shōhin

75. Finances

stock (share)	株	kabu
bond (certificate)	債券	saiken
bill of exchange	為替手形	kawase tegata

| stock exchange | 証券取引所 | shōken torihiki sho |
| stock price | 株価 | kabuka |

| to go down | 安くなる | yasuku naru |
| to go up | 高くなる | takaku naru |

shareholding	株式保有	kabushiki hoyū
controlling interest	企業支配権	kigyō shihai ken
investment	投資	tōshi
to invest (vt)	投資する	tōshi suru
percent	百分率	hyakubunritsu
interest (on investment)	利子	rishi

profit	利益	rieki
profitable (adj)	利益のある	rieki no aru
tax	税	zei

currency (foreign ~)	通貨	tsūka
national (adj)	国の	kuni no
exchange (currency ~)	両替	ryōgae

| accountant | 会計士 | kaikeishi |
| accounting | 会計 | kaikei |

bankruptcy	破産	hasan
collapse, crash	破綻	hatan
ruin	破産	hasan
to be ruined	破産する	hasan suru

| inflation | インフレ | infure |
| devaluation | 平価切り下げ | heika kirisage |

capital	資本	shihon
income	収益	shūeki
turnover	売上高	uriage daka
resources	財源	zaigen
monetary resources	貨幣資産	kahei shisan
overhead	諸経費	shokeihi
to reduce (expenses)	削減する	sakugen suru

76. Marketing

marketing	マーケティング	māketingu
market	市場	shijō
market segment	市場区分	shijō kubun
product	製品	seihin
goods	品物	shinamono
brand	ブランド	burando
trademark	商標	shōhyō
logotype	ロゴタイプ	rogo taipu
logo	ロゴ	rogo
demand	需要	juyō
supply	供給	kyōkyū
need	必要	hitsuyō
consumer	消費者	shōhi sha
analysis	分析	bunseki
to analyze (vt)	分析する	bunseki suru
positioning	ポジショニング	pojishoningu
to position (vt)	ポジショニングする	pojishoningu suru
price	価格	kakaku
pricing policy	価格政策	kakaku seisaku
formation of price	価格形成	kakaku keisei

77. Advertising

advertising	広告	kōkoku
to advertise (vt)	広告する	kōkoku suru
budget	予算	yosan
ad, advertisement	広告	kōkoku
TV advertising	テレビ広告	terebi kōkoku
radio advertising	ラジオ広告	rajio kōkoku
outdoor advertising	屋外広告	okugai kōkoku
mass media	マスメディア	masumedia
periodical (n)	定期刊行物	teiki kankō butsu
image (public appearance)	イメージ	imēji
slogan	スローガン	surōgan
motto (maxim)	モットー	mottō
campaign	キャンペーン	kyanpēn
advertising campaign	広告キャンペーン	kōkoku kyanpēn
target group	ターゲット・オーディエンス	tāgetto ōdiensu

business card	名刺	meishi
leaflet	チラシ	chirashi
brochure	パンフレット	panfuretto
(e.g., 12 pages ~)		
pamphlet	小冊子	shō sasshi
newsletter	ニュースレター	nyūsuretā
store sign	店看板	mise kanban
poster	ポスター	posutā
billboard	広告掲示板	kōkoku keijiban

78. Banking

bank	銀行	ginkō
branch (of bank, etc.)	支店	shiten
bank clerk, consultant	銀行員	ginkōin
manager (director)	長	chō
banking account	口座	kōza
account number	口座番号	kōza bangō
checking account	当座預金口座	tōza yokin kōza
savings account	貯蓄預金口座	chochiku yokin kōza
to open an account	口座を開く	kōza wo hiraku
to close the account	口座を解約する	kōza wo kaiyaku suru
to deposit into the account	口座に預金する	kōza ni yokin suru
to withdraw (vt)	引き出す	hikidasu
deposit	預金	yokin
to make a deposit	預金する	yokin suru
wire transfer	送金	sōkin
to wire, to transfer	送金する	sōkin suru
sum	合計金額	gōkei kingaku
How much?	いくら？	ikura ?
signature	署名	shomei
to sign (vt)	署名する	shomei suru
credit card	クレジットカード	kurejitto kādo
code	コード	kōdo
credit card number	クレジットカード番号	kurejitto kādo bangō
ATM	ATM	ētīemu
check	小切手	kogitte
to write a check	小切手を書く	kogitte wo kaku
checkbook	小切手帳	kogitte chō
loan (bank ~)	融資	yūshi
to apply for a loan	融資を申し込む	yūshi wo mōshikomu

to get a loan	融資を受ける	yūshi wo ukeru
to give a loan	融資を行う	yūshi wo okonau
guarantee	保障	hoshō

79. Telephone. Phone conversation

telephone	電話	denwa
mobile phone	携帯電話	keitai denwa
answering machine	留守番電話	rusuban denwa

| to call (telephone) | 電話する | denwa suru |
| phone call | 電話 | denwa |

to dial a number	電話番号をダイアルする	denwa bangō wo daiaru suru
Hello!	もしもし	moshimoshi
to ask (vt)	問う	tō
to answer (vi, vt)	出る	deru

to hear (vt)	聞く	kiku
well (adv)	良く	yoku
not well (adv)	良くない	yoku nai
noises (interference)	電波障害	denpa shōgai

receiver	受話器	juwaki
to pick up (~ the phone)	電話に出る	denwa ni deru
to hang up (~ the phone)	電話を切る	denwa wo kiru

busy (adj)	話し中	hanashi chū
to ring (ab. phone)	鳴る	naru
telephone book	電話帳	denwa chō

local (adj)	市内の	shinai no
local call	市内電話	shinai denwa
long distance (~ call)	市外の	shigai no
long-distance call	市外電話	shigai denwa
international (adj)	国際の	kokusai no
international call	国際電話	kokusai denwa

80. Mobile telephone

mobile phone	携帯電話	keitai denwa
display	ディスプレイ	disupurei
button	ボタン	botan
SIM card	SIMカード	shimu kādo

| battery | 電池 | denchi |
| to be dead (battery) | 切れる | kireru |

charger	充電器	jūden ki
menu	メニュー	menyū
settings	設定	settei
tune (melody)	メロディー	merodī
to select (vt)	選択する	sentaku suru
calculator	電卓	dentaku
voice mail	ボイスメール	boisu mēru
alarm clock	目覚まし	mezamashi
contacts	連絡先	renraku saki
SMS (text message)	テキストメッセージ	tekisuto messēji
subscriber	加入者	kanyū sha

81. Stationery

ballpoint pen	ボールペン	bōrupen
fountain pen	万年筆	mannenhitsu
pencil	鉛筆	enpitsu
highlighter	蛍光ペン	keikō pen
felt-tip pen	フェルトペン	feruto pen
notepad	メモ帳	memo chō
agenda (diary)	手帳	techō
ruler	定規	jōgi
calculator	電卓	dentaku
eraser	消しゴム	keshigomu
thumbtack	画鋲	gabyō
paper clip	ゼムクリップ	zemu kurippu
glue	糊	nori
stapler	ホッチキス	hocchikisu
hole punch	パンチ	panchi
pencil sharpener	鉛筆削り	enpitsu kezuri

82. Kinds of business

accounting services	会計サービス	kaikei sābisu
advertising	広告	kōkoku
advertising agency	広告代理店	kōkoku dairi ten
air-conditioners	エアコン	eakon
airline	航空会社	kōkū gaisha
alcoholic drinks	アルコール飲料	arukōru inryō
antiquities	骨董品	kottō hin
art gallery	画廊	garō

audit services	監査サービス	kansa sābisu
banks	銀行業	ginkō gyō
bar	バー	bā
beauty parlor	美容院	biyō in
bookstore	本屋	honya
brewery	ビール醸造所	bīru jōzō jo
business center	ビジネスセンター	bijinesu sentā
business school	ビジネススクール	bijinesu sukūru
casino	カジノ	kajino
construction	建設業	kensetsu gyō
consulting	コンサルタント業	konsarutanto gyō
dental clinic	歯科医院	shika īn
design	デザイン	dezain
drugstore, pharmacy	薬局	yakkyoku
dry cleaners	クリーニング屋	kurīningu ya
employment agency	職業紹介所	shokugyō shōkai sho
financial services	金融サービス	kinyū sābisu
food products	食品	shokuhin
funeral home	葬儀社	sōgi sha
furniture (e.g., house ~)	家具	kagu
garment	衣服	ifuku
hotel	ホテル	hoteru
ice-cream	アイスクリーム	aisukurīmu
industry	産業	sangyō
insurance	保険	hoken
Internet	インターネット	intānetto
investment	投資	tōshi
jeweler	宝石商	hōsekishō
jewelry	宝石	hōseki
laundry (shop)	洗濯屋	sentaku ya
legal advisor	法律事務所	hōritsu jimusho
light industry	軽工業	keikōgyō
magazine	雑誌	zasshi
mail-order selling	通信販売	tsūshin hanbai
medicine	医療	iryō
movie theater	映画館	eiga kan
museum	博物館	hakubutsukan
news agency	通信社	tsūshin sha
newspaper	新聞	shinbun
nightclub	ナイトクラブ	naito kurabu
oil (petroleum)	油	abura
parcels service	宅配便	takuhai bin
pharmaceuticals	製薬会社	seiyaku kaisha
printing (industry)	印刷業	insatsu gyō

publishing house	出版社	shuppan sha
radio (~ station)	ラジオ	rajio
real estate	不動産	fudōsan
restaurant	レストラン	resutoran
security agency	警備会社	keibi gaisha
sports	スポーツ	supōtsu
stock exchange	証券取引所	shōken torihiki sho
store	店、…屋	mise, …ya
supermarket	スーパーマーケット	sūpāmāketto
swimming pool	プール	pūru
tailors	仕立て屋	shitateya
television	テレビ	terebi
theater	劇場	gekijō
trade	取引	torihiki
transportation	輸送	yusō
travel	旅行	ryokō
veterinarian	獣医	jūi
warehouse	倉庫	sōko
waste collection	ごみ収集	gomi shūshū

Job. Business. Part 2

83. Show. Exhibition

exhibition, show	博覧会	hakuran kai
trade show	見本市	mihonichi
participation	参加	sanka
to participate (vi)	参加する	sanka suru
participant (exhibitor)	参加者	sanka sha
director	責任者	sekinin sha
organizer's office	事務局	jimu kyoku
organizer	主催者	shusai sha
to organize (vt)	主催する	shusai suru
participation form	申込書	mōshikomi sho
to fill out (vt)	記入する	kinyū suru
details	詳細	shōsai
information	案内	annai
price	出展料	shutten ryō
including	…込み、…を含む	… komi , … wo fukumu
to include (vt)	含める	fukumeru
to pay (vi, vt)	払う	harau
registration fee	登録料	tōroku ryō
entrance	入り口	iriguchi
pavilion, hall	展示館	tenji kan
to register (vt)	登録する	tōroku suru
badge (identity tag)	名札	nafuda
booth, stand	小間、ブース	koma, būsu
to reserve, to book	予約する	yoyaku suru
display case	ショーケース	shōkēsu
spotlight	スポットライト	supottoraito
design	デザイン	dezain
to place (put, set)	置く	oku
to be placed	置かれる	okareru
distributor	代理店	dairi ten
supplier	供給者	kyōkyū sha
to supply (vt)	供給する	kyōkyū suru
country	国	kuni
foreign (adj)	外国の	gaikoku no

product	製品	seihin
association	協会	kyōkai
conference hall	会議場	kaigi jō
congress	会議	kaigi
contest (competition)	コンテスト	kontesuto

visitor	来場者	raijō sha
to visit (attend)	見に行く	mi ni iku
customer	客	kyaku

84. Science. Research. Scientists

science	科学	kagaku
scientific (adj)	科学の	kagaku no
scientist	科学者	kagaku sha
theory	理論	riron

axiom	公理	kōri
analysis	分析	bunseki
to analyze (vt)	分析する	bunseki suru
argument (strong ~)	論拠	ronkyo
substance (matter)	物質	busshitsu

hypothesis	仮説	kasetsu
dilemma	ジレンマ	jirenma
dissertation	論文	ronbun
dogma	定説	teisetsu

doctrine	教義	kyōgi
research	研究	kenkyū
to do research	研究する	kenkyū suru
testing	検査すること	kensa suru koto
laboratory	研究室	kenkyū shitsu

method	方法	hōhō
molecule	分子	bunshi
monitoring	モニタリング	monitaringu
discovery (act, event)	発見	hakken

postulate	仮定	katei
principle	原理	genri
forecast	予想	yosō
prognosticate (vt)	予想する	yosō suru

synthesis	合成	gōsei
trend (tendency)	傾向	keikō
theorem	定理	teiri

| teachings | 教え | oshie |
| fact | 事実 | jijitsu |

expedition	探検	tanken
experiment	実験	jikken
academician	アカデミー会員	akademī kaīn
bachelor (e.g., ~ of Arts)	学士	gakushi
doctor (PhD)	博士	hakase
Associate Professor	准教授	jun kyōju
Master (e.g., ~ of Arts)	修士	shūshi
professor	教授	kyōju

Professions and occupations

85. Job search. Dismissal

job	仕事	shigoto
staff (work force)	部員	buin
personnel	従業員	jyūgyōin
career	職歴	shokureki
prospects	見通し	mitōshi
skills (mastery)	専門技術	senmon gijutsu
selection (screening)	選考	senkō
employment agency	職業紹介所	shokugyō shōkai sho
résumé	履歴書	rireki sho
interview (for job)	面接	mensetsu
vacancy, opening	欠員	ketsuin
salary, pay	給料	kyūryō
fixed salary	固定給	kotei kyū
pay, compensation	給与	kyūyo
position (job)	地位	chī
duty (of employee)	職務	shokumu
range of duties	職務範囲	shokumu hani
busy (I'm ~)	忙しい	isogashī
to fire (dismiss)	解雇する	kaiko suru
dismissal	解雇	kaiko
unemployment	失業	shitsugyō
unemployed (n)	失業者	shitsugyō sha
retirement	退職	taishoku
to retire (from job)	退職する	taishoku suru

86. Business people

director	責任者	sekinin sha
manager (director)	管理者	kanri sha
boss	ボス	bosu
superior	上司	jōshi
superiors	上司	jōshi
president	社長	shachō

chairman	会長	kaichō
deputy (substitute)	副部長	fuku buchō
assistant	助手	joshu
secretary	秘書	hisho
personal assistant	個人秘書	kojin hisho

businessman	ビジネスマン	bijinesuman
entrepreneur	企業家	kigyō ka
founder	創立者	sōritsu sha
to found (vt)	創立する	sōritsu suru

incorporator	共同出資者	kyōdō shusshi sha
partner	パートナー	pātonā
stockholder	株主	kabunushi

millionaire	百万長者	hyakuman chōja
billionaire	億万長者	okuman chōja
owner, proprietor	経営者	keieisha
landowner	土地所有者	tochi shoyū sha

client	クライアント	kuraianto
regular client	常連客	jōren kyaku
buyer (customer)	買い手	kaite
visitor	来客	raikyaku

professional (n)	熟練者	jukuren sha
expert	エキスパート	ekisupāto
specialist	専門家	senmon ka

| banker | 銀行家 | ginkō ka |
| broker | 仲買人 | nakagainin |

cashier, teller	レジ係	reji gakari
accountant	会計士	kaikeishi
security guard	警備員	keibi in

investor	投資者	tōshi sha
debtor	債務者	saimu sha
creditor	債権者	saiken sha
borrower	借り主	karinushi

| importer | 輸入業者 | yunyū gyōsha |
| exporter | 輸出業者 | yushutsu gyōsha |

manufacturer	メーカー	mēkā
distributor	代理店	dairi ten
middleman	中間業者	chūkan gyōsha

consultant	コンサルタント	konsarutanto
sales representative	販売外交員	hanbai gaikōin
agent	代理人	dairinin
insurance agent	保険代理人	hoken dairinin

87. Service professions

cook	料理人	ryōri jin
chef (kitchen chef)	シェフ	shefu
baker	パン職人	pan shokunin
bartender	バーテンダー	bātendā
waiter	ウェイター	weitā
waitress	ウェートレス	wētoresu
lawyer, attorney	弁護士	bengoshi
lawyer (legal expert)	法律顧問	hōritsu komon
notary	公証人	kōshō nin
electrician	電気工事士	denki kōji shi
plumber	配管工	haikan kō
carpenter	大工	daiku
masseur	マッサージ師	massāji shi
masseuse	女性マッサージ師	josei massāji shi
doctor	医者	isha
taxi driver	タクシーの運転手	takushī no unten shu
driver	運転手	unten shu
delivery man	宅配業者	takuhai gyōsha
chambermaid	客室係	kyakushitsu gakari
security guard	警備員	keibi in
flight attendant	客室乗務員	kyakushitsu jōmu in
teacher (in primary school)	教師	kyōshi
librarian	図書館員	toshokan in
translator	翻訳者	honyaku sha
interpreter	通訳者	tsūyaku sha
guide	ガイド	gaido
hairdresser	美容師	biyō shi
mailman	郵便配達人	yūbin haitatsu jin
salesman (store staff)	店員	tenin
gardener	庭師	niwashi
domestic servant	使用人	shiyōnin
maid	メイド	meido
cleaner (cleaning lady)	掃除婦	sōjifu

88. Military professions and ranks

| private | 二等兵 | nitōhei |
| sergeant | 軍曹 | gunsō |

lieutenant	中尉	chūi
captain	大尉	taī
major	少佐	shōsa
colonel	大佐	taisa
general	将官	shōkan
marshal	元帥	gensui
admiral	提督	teitoku
military man	軍人	gunjin
soldier	兵士	heishi
officer	士官	shikan
commander	指揮官	shiki kan
border guard	国境警備兵	kokkyō keibi hei
radio operator	通信士	tsūshin shi
scout (searcher)	斥候	sekkō
pioneer (sapper)	工兵	kōhei
marksman	射手	shashu
navigator	航空士	kōkū shi

89. Officials. Priests

king	国王	kokuō
queen	女王	joō
prince	王子	ōji
princess	王妃	ōhi
tsar, czar	ツァーリ	tsāri
czarina	女帝	nyotei
president	大統領	daitōryō
Secretary (~ of State)	長官	chōkan
prime minister	首相	shushō
senator	上院議員	jōin gīn
diplomat	外交官	gaikō kan
consul	領事	ryōji
ambassador	大使	taishi
advisor (military ~)	顧問	komon
official (civil servant)	公務員	kōmuin
prefect	知事	chiji
mayor	市長	shichō
judge	裁判官	saibankan
district attorney (prosecutor)	検察官	kensatsukan
missionary	宣教師	senkyōshi

monk	修道士	shūdō shi
abbot	修道院長	shūdōin chō
rabbi	ラビ	rabi

vizier	ワズィール	wazīru
shah	シャー	shā
sheikh	シャイフ	shaifu

90. Agricultural professions

beekeeper	養蜂家	yōhōka
herder, shepherd	牛飼い	ushikai
agronomist	農学者	nōgaku sha
cattle breeder	牧畜業者	bokuchiku gyōsha
veterinarian	獣医	jūi

farmer	農業経営者	nōgyō keiei sha
winemaker	ワイン生産者	wain seisan sha
zoologist	動物学者	dōbutsu gakusha
cowboy	カウボーイ	kaubōi

91. Art professions

| actor | 俳優 | haiyū |
| actress | 女優 | joyū |

| singer (masc.) | 歌手 | kashu |
| singer (fem.) | 歌手 | kashu |

| dancer (masc.) | ダンサー | dansā |
| dancer (fem.) | ダンサー | dansā |

| performing artist (masc.) | 芸能人 | geinōjin |
| performing artist (fem.) | 芸能人 | geinōjin |

musician	音楽家	ongakuka
pianist	ピアニスト	pianisuto
guitar player	ギターリスト	gitā risuto

conductor (orchestra ~)	指揮者	shiki sha
composer	作曲家	sakkyoku ka
impresario	マネージャー	manējā

movie director	映画監督	eiga kantoku
producer	プロデューサー	purodyūsā
scriptwriter	台本作家	daihon sakka
critic	評論家	hyōron ka
writer	作家	sakka

poet	詩人	shijin
sculptor	彫刻家	chōkoku ka
artist (painter)	画家	gaka

juggler	手品師	tejina shi
clown	道化師	dōkeshi
acrobat	曲芸師	kyokugei shi
magician	手品師	tejina shi

92. Various professions

doctor	医者	isha
nurse	看護師	kangoshi
psychiatrist	精神科医	seishin kai
dentist	歯科医	shikai
surgeon	外科医	gekai

astronaut	宇宙飛行士	uchū hikō shi
astronomer	天文学者	tenmongaku sha
pilot	パイロット	pairotto

driver (of taxi, etc.)	運転手	unten shu
engineer (train driver)	機関士	kikan shi
mechanic	修理士	shūri shi

miner	鉱山労働者	kōzan rōdō sha
worker	労働者	rōdō sha
metalworker	金工	kinkō
joiner (carpenter)	家具大工	kagu daiku
turner	旋盤工	senban kō
construction worker	建設作業員	kensetsu sagyō in
welder	溶接工	yōsetsu kō

professor (title)	教授	kyōju
architect	建築士	kenchiku shi
historian	歴史家	rekishi ka
scientist	科学者	kagaku sha
physicist	物理学者	butsuri gakusha
chemist (scientist)	化学者	kagaku sha

archeologist	考古学者	kōkogakusha
geologist	地質学者	chishitsu gakusha
researcher	研究者	kenkyū sha

| babysitter | ベビーシッター | bebīshittā |
| teacher, educator | 教育者 | kyōiku sha |

editor	編集者	henshū sha
editor-in-chief	編集長	henshū chō
correspondent	特派員	tokuhain

typist (fem.)	タイピスト	taipisuto
designer	デザイナー	dezainā
computer expert	コンピュータ専門家	konpyūta senmon ka
programmer	プログラマー	puroguramā
engineer (designer)	技師	gishi

sailor	水夫	suifu
seaman	船員	senin
rescuer	救助員	kyūjo in

fireman	消防士	shōbō shi
policeman	警官	keikan
watchman	警備員	keibi in
detective	探偵	tantei

customs officer	税関吏	zeikanri
bodyguard	ボディーガード	bodīgādo
prison guard	刑務官	keimu kan
inspector	検査官	kensakan

sportsman	スポーツマン	supōtsuman
trainer, coach	トレーナー	torēnā
butcher	肉屋	nikuya
cobbler	靴修理屋	kutsu shūri ya
merchant	商人	shōnin
loader (person)	荷役作業員	niyakusa gyōin

| fashion designer | ファッションデザイナー | fasshon dezainā |
| model (fem.) | モデル | moderu |

93. Occupations. Social status

| schoolboy | 男子生徒 | danshi seito |
| student (college ~) | 学生 | gakusei |

philosopher	哲学者	tetsu gakusha
economist	経済学者	keizai gakusha
inventor	発明者	hatsumei sha

unemployed (n)	失業者	shitsugyō sha
retiree	退職者	taishoku sha
spy, secret agent	スパイ	supai

prisoner	囚人	shūjin
striker	ストライキをする人	sutoraiki wo suru hito
bureaucrat	官僚主義者	kanryō shugi sha
traveler	旅行者	ryokō sha

| homosexual | 同性愛者 | dōseiai sha |
| hacker | ハッカー | hakkā |

hippie	ヒッピー	hippī
bandit	山賊	sanzoku
hit man, killer	殺し屋	koroshi ya
drug addict	麻薬中毒者	mayaku chūdoku sha
drug dealer	麻薬の売人	mayaku no bainin
prostitute (fem.)	売春婦	baishun fu
pimp	ポン引き	pon biki
sorcerer	魔法使い	mahōtsukai
sorceress	女魔法使い	jo mahōtsukai
pirate	海賊	kaizoku
slave	奴隷	dorei
samurai	侍、武士	samurai, bushi
savage (primitive)	未開人	mikai jin

Education

94. School

school	学校	gakkō
headmaster	校長	kōchō
pupil (boy)	生徒	seito
pupil (girl)	女生徒	jo seito
schoolboy	男子生徒	danshi seito
schoolgirl	女子生徒	joshi seito
to teach (sb)	教える	oshieru
to learn (language, etc.)	学ぶ	manabu
to learn by heart	暗記する	anki suru
to study (work to learn)	勉強する	benkyō suru
to be in school	学校に通う	gakkō ni kayō
to go to school	学校へ行く	gakkō he iku
alphabet	アルファベット	arufabetto
subject (at school)	科目	kamoku
classroom	教室	kyōshitsu
lesson	レッスン	ressun
recess	休み時間	yasumi jikan
school bell	ベル	beru
school desk	学校用机	gakkō yō tsukue
chalkboard	黒板	kokuban
grade	成績	seiseki
good grade	良い成績	yoi seiseki
bad grade	悪い成績	warui seiseki
to give a grade	成績を付ける	seiseki wo tsukeru
mistake, error	間違い	machigai
to make mistakes	間違える	machigaeru
to correct (an error)	直す	naosu
cheat sheet	カンニングペーパー	kanningu pēpā
homework	宿題	shukudai
exercise (in education)	練習	renshū
to be present	出席する	shusseki suru
to be absent	欠席する	kesseki suru
to miss school	学校を休む	gakkō wo yasumu

to punish (vt)	罰する	bassuru
punishment	罰	batsu
conduct (behavior)	行動	kōdō

report card	通信簿	tsūshin bo
pencil	鉛筆	enpitsu
eraser	消しゴム	keshigomu
chalk	チョーク	chōku
pencil case	筆箱	fudebako

schoolbag	通学カバン	tsūgaku kaban
pen	ペン	pen
school notebook	ノート	nōto
textbook	教科書	kyōkasho
compasses	コンパス	konpasu

| to draw (a blueprint, etc.) | 製図する | seizu suru |
| technical drawing | 製図 | seizu |

poem	詩	shi
by heart (adv)	暗記して	anki shi te
to learn by heart	暗記する	anki suru

school vacation	休暇	kyūka
to be on vacation	休暇中である	kyūka chū de aru
to spend one's vacation	休暇を過ごす	kyūka wo sugosu

test (written math ~)	筆記試験	hikki shiken
essay (composition)	論文式試験	ronbun shiki shiken
dictation	書き取り	kakitori
exam	試験	shiken
to take an exam	試験を受ける	shiken wo ukeru
experiment (chemical ~)	実験	jikken

95. College. University

academy	アカデミー	akademī
university	大学	daigaku
faculty (section)	学部	gakubu

student (masc.)	学生	gakusei
student (fem.)	学生	gakusei
lecturer (teacher)	講師	kōshi

lecture hall, room	講堂	kōdō
graduate	卒業生	sotsugyōsei
diploma	卒業証書	sotsugyō shōsho
dissertation	論文	ronbun
study (report)	研究書	kenkyū sho
laboratory	研究室	kenkyū shitsu

lecture	講義	kōgi
course mate	同級生	dōkyūsei
scholarship	奨学金	shōgaku kin
academic degree	学位	gakui

96. Sciences. Disciplines

mathematics	数学	sūgaku
algebra	代数学	daisūgaku
geometry	幾何学	kikagaku

astronomy	天文学	tenmon gaku
biology	生物学	seibutsu gaku
geography	地理学	chiri gaku
geology	地質学	chishitsu gaku
history	歴史	rekishi

medicine	医学	igaku
pedagogy	教育学	kyōiku gaku
law	法学	hōgaku

physics	物理学	butsuri gaku
chemistry	化学	kagaku
philosophy	哲学	tetsugaku
psychology	心理学	shinrigaku

97. Writing system. Orthography

grammar	文法	bunpō
vocabulary	語彙	goi
phonetics	音声学	onseigaku

| noun | 名詞 | meishi |
| adjective | 形容詞 | keiyōshi |

| verb | 動詞 | dōshi |
| adverb | 副詞 | fukushi |

pronoun	代名詞	daimeishi
interjection	間投詞	kantōshi
preposition	前置詞	zenchishi

root	語根	gokon
ending	語尾	gobi
prefix	接頭辞	settō ji
syllable	音節	onsetsu
suffix	接尾辞	setsubi ji
stress mark	キョウセイ [強勢]	kyōsei

apostrophe	アポストロフィー	aposutorofī
period, dot	句点	kuten
comma	コンマ	konma
semicolon	セミコロン	semikoron

| colon | コロン | koron |
| ellipsis | 省略 | shōrya ku |

| question mark | 疑問符 | gimon fu |
| exclamation point | 感嘆符 | kantan fu |

| quotation marks | 引用符 | inyō fu |
| in quotation marks | 引用符内 | inyō fu nai |

| parenthesis | ガッコ（括弧） | gakko |
| in parenthesis | ガッコ内 （括弧内） | kakko nai |

hyphen	ハイフン	haifun
dash	ダッシュ	dasshu
space (between words)	スペース	supēsu

| letter | 文字 | moji |
| capital letter | 大文字 | daimonji |

| vowel (n) | 母音 | boin |
| consonant (n) | 子音 | shīn |

sentence	文	bun
subject	主語	shugo
predicate	述語	jutsugo

line	行	gyō
on a new line	新しい行で	atarashī gyō de
paragraph	段落	danraku

word	単語	tango
group of words	語群	gogun
expression	表現	hyōgen

| synonym | 同義語 | dōgigo |
| antonym | 対義語 | taigigo |

rule	規則	kisoku
exception	例外	reigai
correct (adj)	正しい	tadashī

conjugation	活用	katsuyō
declension	語形変化	gokei henka
nominal case	名詞格	meishi kaku
question	疑問文	gimon bun
to underline (vt)	下線を引く	kasen wo hiku
dotted line	点線	tensen

98. Foreign languages

language	言語	gengo
foreign (adj)	外国の	gaikoku no
foreign language	外国語	gaikoku go
to study (vt)	勉強する	benkyō suru
to learn (language, etc.)	学ぶ	manabu
to read (vi, vt)	読む	yomu
to speak (vi, vt)	話す	hanasu
to understand (vt)	理解する	rikai suru
to write (vt)	書く	kaku
fast (adv)	速く	hayaku
slowly (adv)	ゆっくり	yukkuri
fluently (adv)	流ちょうに	ryūchō ni
rules	規則	kisoku
grammar	文法	bunpō
vocabulary	語彙	goi
phonetics	音声学	onseigaku
textbook	教科書	kyōkasho
dictionary	辞書	jisho
teach-yourself book	独習書	dokushū sho
phrasebook	慣用表現集	kanyō hyōgen shū
cassette	カセットテープ	kasettotēpu
videotape	ビデオテープ	bideotēpu
CD, compact disc	CD（シーディー）	shīdī
DVD	DVD［ディーブイディー］	dībuidī
alphabet	アルファベット	arufabetto
to spell (vt)	スペリングを言う	superingu wo iu
pronunciation	発音	hatsuon
accent	なまり［訛り］	namari
with an accent	訛りのある	namari no aru
without an accent	訛りのない	namari no nai
word	単語	tango
meaning	意味	imi
course (e.g., a French ~)	講座	kōza
to sign up	申し込む	mōshikomu
teacher	先生	sensei
translation (process)	翻訳	honyaku
translation (text, etc.)	訳文	yakubun
translator	翻訳者	honyaku sha
interpreter	通訳者	tsūyaku sha

| polyglot | ポリグロット | porigurotto |
| memory | 記憶 | kioku |

Rest. Entertainment. Travel

99. Trip. Travel

tourism	観光	kankō
tourist	観光客	kankō kyaku
trip, voyage	旅行	ryokō
adventure	冒険	bōken
trip, journey	旅	tabi
vacation	休暇	kyūka
to be on vacation	休暇中です	kyūka chū desu
rest	休み	yasumi
train	列車	ressha
by train	列車で	ressha de
airplane	航空機	kōkūki
by airplane	飛行機で	hikōki de
by car	車で	kuruma de
by ship	船で	fune de
luggage	荷物	nimotsu
suitcase, luggage	スーツケース	sūtsukēsu
luggage cart	荷物カート	nimotsu kāto
passport	パスポート	pasupōto
visa	ビザ	biza
ticket	乗車券	jōsha ken
air ticket	航空券	kōkū ken
guidebook	ガイドブック	gaido bukku
map	地図	chizu
area (rural ~)	地域	chīki
place, site	場所	basho
exotic (n)	エキゾチック	ekizochikku
exotic (adj)	エキゾチックな	ekizochikku na
amazing (adj)	驚くべき	odoroku beki
group	団	dan
excursion	小旅行	shō ryokō
guide (person)	ツアーガイド	tuā gaido

100. Hotel

hotel	ホテル	hoteru
motel	モーテル	mō teru
three-star	三つ星	mitsu boshi
five-star	五つ星	itsutsu boshi
to stay (in hotel, etc.)	泊まる	tomaru
room	部屋、ルーム	heya, rūmu
single room	シングルルーム	shinguru rūmu
double room	ダブルルーム	daburu rūmu
to book a room	部屋を予約する	heya wo yoyaku suru
half board	ハーフボード	hāfu bōdo
full board	フルボード	furu bōdo
with bath	浴槽付きの	yokusō tsuki no
with shower	シャワー付きの	shawā tsuki no
satellite television	衛星テレビ	eisei terebi
air-conditioner	エアコン	eakon
towel	タオル	taoru
key	鍵	kagi
administrator	管理人	kanri jin
chambermaid	客室係	kyakushitsu gakari
porter, bellboy	ベルボーイ	beru bōi
doorman	ドアマン	doa man
restaurant	レストラン	resutoran
pub, bar	パブ、バー	pabu, bā
breakfast	朝食	chōshoku
dinner	夕食	yūshoku
buffet	ビュッフェ	byuffe
lobby	ロビー	robī
elevator	エレベーター	erebētā
DO NOT DISTURB	起こさないで下さい	okosa nai de kudasai
NO SMOKING	禁煙	kinen

TECHNICAL EQUIPMENT. TRANSPORTATION

Technical equipment

101. Computer

computer	コンピューター	konpyūtā
notebook, laptop	ノートパソコン	nōto pasokon
to turn on	入れる	ireru
to turn off	消す	kesu
keyboard	キーボード	kībōdo
key	キー	kī
mouse	マウス	mausu
mouse pad	マウスパッド	mausu paddo
button	ボタン	botan
cursor	カーソル	kāsoru
monitor	モニター	monitā
screen	スクリーン	sukurīn
hard disk	ハードディスク	hādo disuku
hard disk volume	ハードディスクの容量	hādo disuku no yōryō
memory	メモリ	memori
random access memory	ランダム・アクセス・メモリ	randamu akusesu memori
file	ファイル	fairu
folder	フォルダ	foruda
to open (vt)	開く	hiraku
to close (vt)	閉じる	tojiru
to save (vt)	保存する	hozon suru
to delete (vt)	削除する	sakujo suru
to copy (vt)	コピーする	kopī suru
to sort (vt)	ソートする	sōto suru
to transfer (copy)	転送する	tensō suru
program	プログラム	puroguramu
software	ソフトウェア	sofutowea
programmer	プログラマ	puroguramu
to program (vt)	プログラムを作る	puroguramu wo tsukuru
hacker	ハッカー	hakkā

password	パスワード	pasuwādo
virus	ウイルス	uirusu
to find, to detect	検出する	kenshutsu suru

| byte | バイト | baito |
| megabyte | メガバイト | megabaito |

| data | データ | dēta |
| database | データベース | dētabēsu |

cable (USB, etc.)	ケーブル	kēburu
to disconnect (vt)	接続を切る	setsuzoku wo kiru
to connect (sth to sth)	接続する	setsuzoku suru

102. Internet. E-mail

Internet	インターネット	intānetto
browser	ブラウザー	burauzā
search engine	検索エンジン	kensaku enjin
provider	プロバイダー	purobaidā

web master	ウェブマスター	webumasutā
website	ウェブサイト	webusaito
web page	ウェブページ	webupēji

| address | アドレス | adoresu |
| address book | 住所録 | jūsho roku |

mailbox	メールボックス	mēru bokkusu
mail	メール	mēru
full (adj)	いっぱい（一杯）	ippai

message	メッセージ	messēji
incoming messages	受信メッセージ	jushin messēji
outgoing messages	送信メッセージ	sōshin messēji
sender	送信者	sōshin sha
to send (vt)	送信する	sōshin suru
sending (of mail)	送信	sōshin

| receiver | 受信者 | jushin sha |
| to receive (vt) | 受信する | jushin suru |

| correspondence | やり取り | yaritori |
| to correspond (vi) | 連絡する | renraku suru |

file	ファイル	fairu
to download (vt)	ダウンロードする	daunrōdo suru
to create (vt)	作成する	sakusei suru
to delete (vt)	削除する	sakujo suru
deleted (adj)	削除された	sakujo sare ta

connection (ADSL, etc.)	接続	setsuzoku
speed	速度	sokudo
modem	モデム	modemu
access	アクセス	akusesu
port (e.g., input ~)	ポート	pōto
connection (make a ~)	接続	setsuzoku
to connect to … (vi)	…に接続する	… ni setsuzoku suru
to select (vt)	選択する	sentaku suru
to search (for …)	検索する	kensaku suru

103. Electricity

electricity	電気	denki
electrical (adj)	電気の	denki no
electric power station	発電所	hatsuden sho
energy	エネルギー	enerugī
electric power	電力	denryoku
light bulb	電球	denkyū
flashlight	懐中電灯	kaichū dentō
street light	街灯	gaitō
light	電灯	dentō
to turn on	つける	tsukeru
to turn off	消す	kesu
to turn off the light	電気を消す	denki wo kesu
to burn out (vi)	切れる	kireru
short circuit	短絡	tanraku
broken wire	断線	dansen
contact	接触	sesshoku
light switch	スイッチ	suicchi
wall socket	コンセント	konsento
plug	プラグ	puragu
extension cord	延長コード	enchō kōdo
fuse	ヒューズ	hyūzu
cable, wire	電線、ケーブル	densen, kēburu
wiring	電気配線	denki haisen
ampere	アンペア	anpea
amperage	アンペア数	anpea sū
volt	ボルト	boruto
voltage	電圧	denatsu
electrical device	電気製品	denki seihin
indicator	表示器	hyōji ki

electrician	電気工事士	denki kōji shi
to solder (vt)	はんだ付けする	handa tsuke suru
soldering iron	半田ごて [はんだごて]	handa gote
electric current	電流	denryū

104. Tools

tool, instrument	道具	dōgu
tools	工具	kōgu
equipment (factory ~)	機器	kiki

hammer	金槌 [金づち]	kanazuchi
screwdriver	ドライバー	doraibā
ax	斧 [おの]	ono

saw	のこぎり	nokogiri
to saw (vt)	のこぎりで切る	nokogiri de kiru
plane (tool)	かんな	kanna
to plane (vt)	かんなをかける	kanna wo kakeru
soldering iron	半田ごて [はんだごて]	handa gote
to solder (vt)	はんだ付けする	handa tsuke suru

file (for metal)	やすり	ya suri
carpenter pincers	カーペンタープライヤー	kāpentā puraiyā
lineman's pliers	ペンチ	penchi
chisel	のみ	nomi

drill bit	ドリルビット	doriru bitto
electric drill	電気ドリル	denki doriru
to drill (vi, vt)	穴を開ける	ana wo akeru

knife	ナイフ	naifu
pocket knife	小型ナイフ	kogata naifu
folding (~ knife)	フォールディング	fōrudingu
blade	刃	ha

sharp (blade, etc.)	鋭い	surudoi
blunt (adj)	鈍い	nibui
to become blunt	鈍る	niburu
to sharpen (vt)	研ぐ	togu

bolt	ボルト	boruto
nut	ナット	natto
thread (of a screw)	ねじ山	nejiyama
wood screw	木ねじ	mokuneji

nail	釘 [くぎ]	kugi
nailhead	釘頭	kugi atama
ruler (for measuring)	定規	jōgi
tape measure	巻き尺	makijaku

spirit level	水準器	suijun ki
magnifying glass	ルーペ	rūpe
measuring instrument	測定道具	sokutei dōgu
to measure (vt)	測る	hakaru
scale (of thermometer, etc.)	目盛り	memori
readings	検針値	kenshin chi
compressor	コンプレッサー	konpuressā
microscope	顕微鏡	kenbikyō
pump (e.g., water ~)	ポンプ	ponpu
robot	ロボット	robotto
laser	レーザー	rēzā
wrench	スパナ	supana
adhesive tape	粘着テープ	nenchaku tēpu
glue	糊	nori
emery paper	紙やすり	kami ya suri
spring	スプリング	supuringu
magnet	磁石	jishaku
gloves	手袋	tebukuro
rope	ロープ	rōpu
cord	紐	himo
wire (e.g., telephone ~)	電線	densen
cable	ケーブル	kēburu
sledgehammer	大ハンマー	dai hanmā
crowbar	バール	bāru
ladder	梯子 [はしご]	hashigo
stepladder	脚立	kyatatsu
to screw (tighten)	締める	shimeru
to unscrew, untwist (vt)	緩める	yurumeru
to tighten (vt)	堅く締める	kataku shimeru
to glue, to stick	接着する	secchaku suru
to cut (vt)	切る	kiru
malfunction (fault)	故障	koshō
repair (mending)	修理	shūri
to repair, to mend (vt)	修理する	shūri suru
to adjust (machine, etc.)	調整する	chōsei suru
to check (to examine)	検査する	kensa suru
checking	検査	kensa
readings	検針値	kenshin chi
reliable (machine)	信頼性の	shinrai sei no
complicated (adj)	複雑な	fukuzatsu na

to rust (get rusted)	さびる ［錆びる］	sabiru
rusty, rusted (adj)	さびた ［錆びた］	sabi ta
rust	さび ［錆］	sabi

Transportation

105. Airplane

airplane	航空機	kōkūki
air ticket	航空券	kōkū ken
airline	航空会社	kōkū gaisha
airport	空港	kūkō
supersonic (adj)	超音速の	chō onsoku no
captain	機長	kichō
crew	乗務員	jōmu in
pilot	パイロット	pairotto
flight attendant	客室乗務員	kyakushitsu jōmu in
navigator	航空士	kōkū shi
wings	翼	tsubasa
tail	尾部	o bu
cockpit	コックピット	kokkupitto
engine	エンジン	enjin
undercarriage	着陸装置	chakuriku sōchi
turbine	タービン	tābin
propeller	プロペラ	puropera
black box	ブラックボックス	burakku bokkusu
control column	操縦ハンドル	sōjū handoru
fuel	燃料	nenryō
safety card	安全のしおり	anzen no shiori
oxygen mask	酸素マスク	sanso masuku
uniform	制服	seifuku
life vest	ライフジャケット	raifu jaketto
parachute	落下傘	rakkasan
takeoff	離陸	ririku
to take off (vi)	離陸する	ririku suru
runway	滑走路	kassō ro
visibility	視程	shitei
flight (act of flying)	飛行	hikō
altitude	高度	kōdo
air pocket	エアポケット	eapoketto
seat	席	seki
headphones	ヘッドホン	heddohon
folding tray	折りたたみ式のテーブル	oritatami shiki no tēburu

| airplane window | 機窓 | kisō |
| aisle | 通路 | tsūro |

106. Train

train	列車	ressha
suburban train	通勤列車	tsūkin ressha
express train	高速鉄道	kōsoku tetsudō
diesel locomotive	ディーゼル機関車	dīzeru kikan sha
steam engine	蒸気機関車	jōki kikan sha
passenger car	客車	kyakusha
dining car	食堂車	shokudō sha
rails	レール	rēru
railroad	鉄道	tetsudō
railway tie	枕木	makuragi
platform (railway ~)	ホーム	hōmu
track (~ 1, 2, etc.)	線路	senro
semaphore	鉄道信号機	tetsudō shingō ki
station	駅	eki
engineer	機関士	kikan shi
porter (of luggage)	ポーター	pōtā
train steward	車掌	shashō
passenger	乗客	jōkyaku
conductor	検札係	kensatsu gakari
corridor (in train)	通路	tsūro
emergency break	非常ブレーキ	hijō burēki
compartment	コンパートメント	konpātomento
berth	寝台	shindai
upper berth	上段寝台	jōdan shindai
lower berth	下段寝台	gedan shindai
bed linen	リネン	rinen
ticket	乗車券	jōsha ken
schedule	時刻表	jikoku hyō
information display	発車標	hassha shirube
to leave, to depart	発車する	hassha suru
departure (of train)	発車	hassha
to arrive (ab. train)	到着する	tōchaku suru
arrival	到着	tōchaku
to arrive by train	電車で来る	densha de kuru
to get on the train	電車に乗る	densha ni noru
to get off the train	電車をおりる	densha wo oriru

train wreck	鉄道事故	tetsudō jiko
to be derailed	脱線する	dassen suru
steam engine	蒸気機関車	jōki kikan sha
stoker, fireman	火夫	kafu
firebox	火室	kashitsu
coal	石炭	sekitan

107. Ship

ship	船舶	senpaku
vessel	大型船	ōgata sen
steamship	蒸気船	jōki sen
riverboat	川船	kawabune
ocean liner	遠洋定期船	enyō teiki sen
cruiser	クルーザー	kurūzā
yacht	ヨット	yotto
tugboat	曳船	eisen
barge	艀、バージ	hashike, bāji
ferry	フェリー	ferī
sailing ship	帆船	hansen
brigantine	ブリガンティン	burigantin
ice breaker	砕氷船	saihyō sen
submarine	潜水艦	sensui kan
boat (flat-bottomed ~)	ボート	bōto
dinghy	ディンギー	dingī
lifeboat	救命艇	kyūmei tei
motorboat	モーターボート	mōtābōto
captain	船長	senchō
seaman	船員	senin
sailor	水夫	suifu
crew	乗組員	norikumi in
boatswain	ボースン	bōsun
ship's boy	キャビンボーイ	kyabin bōi
cook	船のコック	fune no kokku
ship's doctor	船医	seni
deck	甲板	kanpan
mast	マスト	masuto
sail	帆	ho
hold	船倉	funagura
bow (prow)	船首	senshu
stern	船尾	senbi
oar	櫂	kai

screw propeller	プロペラ	puropera
cabin	船室	senshitsu
wardroom	士官室	shikan shitsu
engine room	機関室	kikan shitsu
bridge	船橋	funabashi
radio room	無線室	musen shitsu
wave (radio)	電波	denpa
logbook	航海日誌	kōkai nisshi
spyglass	単眼望遠鏡	tangan bōenkyō
bell	船鐘	funekane
flag	旗	hata
rope (mooring ~)	ロープ	rōpu
knot (bowline, etc.)	結び目	musubime
deckrail	手摺	tesuri
gangway	舷門	genmon
anchor	錨 [いかり]	ikari
to weigh anchor	錨をあげる	ikari wo ageru
to drop anchor	錨を下ろす	ikari wo orosu
anchor chain	錨鎖	byōsa
port (harbor)	港	minato
berth, wharf	埠頭	futō
to berth (moor)	係留する	keiryū suru
to cast off	出航する	shukkō suru
trip, voyage	旅行	ryokō
cruise (sea trip)	クルーズ	kurūzu
course (route)	針路	shinro
route (itinerary)	船のルート	fune no rūto
fairway	航路	kōro
shallows (shoal)	浅瀬	asase
to run aground	浅瀬に乗り上げる	asase ni noriageru
storm	嵐	arashi
signal	信号	shingō
to sink (vi)	沈没する	chinbotsu suru
Man overboard!	落水したぞ！	ochimizu shi ta zo!
SOS	SOS	
ring buoy	救命浮輪	kyūmei ukiwa

108. Airport

airport	空港	kūkō
airplane	航空機	kōkūki
airline	航空会社	kōkū gaisha

air-traffic controller	航空管制官	kōkū kansei kan
departure	出発	shuppatsu
arrival	到着	tōchaku
to arrive (by plane)	到着する	tōchaku suru

| departure time | 出発時刻 | shuppatsu jikoku |
| arrival time | 到着時刻 | tōchaku jikoku |

| to be delayed | 遅れる | okureru |
| flight delay | フライトの遅延 | furaito no chien |

information board	フライト情報	furaito jōhō
information	案内	annai
to announce (vt)	アナウンスする	anaunsu suru
flight (e.g., next ~)	フライト	furaito

| customs | 税関 | zeikan |
| customs officer | 税関吏 | zeikanri |

customs declaration	税関申告	zeikan shinkoku
to fill out (vt)	記入する	kinyū suru
to fill out the declaration	申告書を記入する	shinkoku sho wo kinyū suru

| passport control | 入国審査 | nyūkoku shinsa |

luggage	荷物	nimotsu
hand luggage	持ち込み荷物	mochikomi nimotsu
Lost Luggage Desk	荷物紛失窓口	nimotsu funshitsu madoguchi

| luggage cart | 荷物カート | nimotsu kāto |

landing	着陸	chakuriku
landing strip	滑走路	kassō ro
to land (vi)	着陸する	chakuriku suru
airstairs	タラップ	tarappu

check-in	チェックイン	chekkuin
check-in desk	チェックインカウンター	chekkuin kauntā
to check-in (vi)	チェックインする	chekkuin suru
boarding pass	搭乗券	tōjō ken
departure gate	出発ゲート	shuppatsu gēto

transit	乗り継ぎ	noritsugi
to wait (vt)	待つ	matsu
departure lounge	出発ロビー	shuppatsu robī
to see off	見送る	miokuru
to say goodbye	別れを告げる	wakare wo tsugeru

Life events

109. Holidays. Event

celebration, holiday	祝日	shukujitsu
national day	国民の祝日	kokumin no shukujitsu
public holiday	公休	kōkyū
to commemorate (vt)	記念する	kinen suru
event (happening)	出来事	dekigoto
event (organized activity)	イベント	ibento
banquet (party)	宴会	enkai
reception (formal party)	レセプション	resepushon
feast	ご馳走 [ごちそう]	gochisō
anniversary	記念日	kinen bi
jubilee	ジュビリー	jubirī
to celebrate (vt)	祝う	iwau
New Year	元日	ganjitsu
Happy New Year!	明けましておめでとうございます	akemashite omedetō gozaimasu
Santa Claus	サンタクロース	santa kurōsu
Christmas	クリスマス	kurisumasu
Merry Christmas!	メリークリスマス！	merī kurisumasu!
Christmas tree	クリスマスツリー	kurisumasutsurī
fireworks	花火	hanabi
wedding	結婚式	kekkonshiki
groom	花婿	hanamuko
bride	花嫁	hanayome
to invite (vt)	招待する	shōtai suru
invitation card	招待状	shōtai jō
guest	客	kyaku
to visit (~ your parents, etc.)	訪ねる	tazuneru
to greet the guests	来客を迎える	raikyaku wo mukaeru
gift, present	贈り物、プレゼント	okurimono, purezento
to give (sth as present)	おくる（贈る）	okuru
to receive gifts	プレゼントをもらう	purezento wo morau
bouquet (of flowers)	花束	hanataba
congratulations	祝辞	shukuji

to congratulate (vt)	祝う	iwau
greeting card	グリーティングカード	gurītingu kādo
to send a postcard	はがきを送る	hagaki wo okuru
to get a postcard	はがきを受け取る	hagaki wo uketoru
toast	祝杯	shukuhai
to offer (a drink, etc.)	…に一杯おごる	… ni ippai ogoru
champagne	シャンパン	shanpan
to have fun	楽しむ	tanoshimu
fun, merriment	歓楽	kanraku
joy (emotion)	喜び	yorokobi
dance	ダンス	dansu
to dance (vi, vt)	踊る	odoru
waltz	ワルツ	warutsu
tango	タンゴ	tango

110. Funerals. Burial

cemetery	墓地	bochi
grave, tomb	墓	haka
cross	十字架	jūjika
gravestone	墓石	boseki
fence	柵	saku
chapel	チャペル	chaperu
death	死	shi
to die (vi)	死ぬ	shinu
the deceased	死者	shisha
mourning	喪	mo
to bury (vt)	葬る	hōmuru
funeral home	葬儀社	sōgi sha
funeral	葬儀	sōgi
wreath	葬式の花輪	sōshiki no hanawa
casket	棺	hitsugi
hearse	霊柩車	reikyūsha
shroud	埋葬布	maisō nuno
funeral procession	葬列	sōretsu
cremation urn	骨壷	kotsutsubo
crematory	火葬場	kasō jō
obituary	死亡記事	shibō kiji
to cry (weep)	泣く	naku
to sob (vi)	むせび泣く	musebinaku

14

111. War. Soldiers

platoon	小隊	shōtai
company	中隊	chūtai
regiment	連隊	rentai
army	陸軍	rikugun
division	師団	shidan
section, squad	分隊	buntai
host (army)	軍隊	guntai
soldier	兵士	heishi
officer	士官	shikan
private	二等兵	nitōhei
sergeant	軍曹	gunsō
lieutenant	中尉	chūi
captain	大尉	taī
major	少佐	shōsa
colonel	大佐	taisa
general	将官	shōkan
sailor	水兵	suihei
captain	艦長	kanchō
boatswain	ボースン	bōsun
artilleryman	砲兵	hōhei
paratrooper	落下傘兵	rakkasan hei
pilot	パイロット	pairotto
navigator	航空士	kōkū shi
mechanic	整備士	seibi shi
pioneer (sapper)	地雷工兵	jirai kōhei
parachutist	落下傘兵	rakkasan hei
reconnaissance scout	偵察斥候	teisatsu sekkō
sniper	狙撃兵	sogeki hei
patrol (group)	パトロール	patorōru
to patrol (vt)	パトロールする	patorōru suru
sentry, guard	番兵	banpei
warrior	戦士	senshi
hero	英雄	eiyū
heroine	英雄	eiyū
patriot	愛国者	aikoku sha
traitor	裏切り者	uragirimono
to betray (vt)	裏切る	uragiru
deserter	脱走兵	dassō hei
to desert (vi)	脱走する	dassō suru
mercenary	傭兵	yōhei

| recruit | 新兵 | shinpei |
| volunteer | 志願兵 | shigan hei |

dead (n)	死者	shisha
wounded (n)	負傷者	fushō sha
prisoner of war	捕虜	horyo

112. War. Military actions. Part 1

war	戦争	sensō
to be at war	戦争中である	sensō chū de aru
civil war	内戦	naisen

treacherously (adv)	裏切って	uragitte
declaration of war	宣戦布告	sensen fukoku
to declare (~ war)	布告する	fukoku suru
aggression	武力侵略	buryoku shinrya ku
to attack (invade)	攻撃する	kōgeki suru

to invade (vt)	侵略する	shinrya ku suru
invader	侵略軍	shinrya ku gun
conqueror	征服者	seifuku sha

| defense | 防衛 | bōei |
| to defend (a country, etc.) | 防衛する | bōei suru |

enemy	敵	teki
foe, adversary	かたき	kataki
enemy (as adj)	敵の	teki no

| strategy | 戦略 | senryaku |
| tactics | 戦術 | senjutsu |

order	命令	meirei
command (order)	命令	meirei
to order (vt)	命令する	meirei suru
mission	任務	ninmu
secret (adj)	秘密の	himitsu no

| battle | 戦い | tatakai |
| combat | 戦闘 | sentō |

attack	攻撃	kōgeki
storming (assault)	突入	totsunyū
to storm (vt)	突入する	totsunyū suru
siege (to be under ~)	包囲	hōi

offensive (n)	攻勢	kōsei
to go on the offensive	攻勢に出る	kōsei ni deru
retreat	撤退	tettai

to retreat (vi)	撤退する	tettai suru
encirclement	包囲	hōi
to encircle (vt)	包囲する	hōi suru
bombing (by aircraft)	爆撃	bakugeki
to drop a bomb	爆弾を投下する	bakudan wo tōka suru
to bomb (vt)	爆撃する	bakugeki suru
explosion	爆発	bakuhatsu
shot	発砲	happō
to fire a shot	発砲する	happō suru
firing (burst of ~)	砲火	hōka
to take aim (at …)	狙う	nerau
to point (a gun)	向ける	mukeru
to hit (the target)	命中する	meichū suru
to sink (~ a ship)	撃沈する	gekichin suru
hole (in a ship)	穴	ana
to founder, to sink (vi)	沈没する	chinbotsu suru
front (war ~)	戦線	sensen
rear (homefront)	銃後	jūgo
evacuation	避難	hinan
to evacuate (vt)	避難する	hinan suru
trench	塹壕	zangō
barbwire	有刺鉄線	yūshitessen
barrier (anti tank ~)	障害物	shōgai butsu
watchtower	監視塔	kanshi tō
hospital	軍病院	gun byōin
to wound (vt)	負傷させる	fushō saseru
wound	負傷	fushō
wounded (n)	負傷者	fushō sha
to be wounded	負傷する	fushō suru
serious (wound)	重い	omoi

113. War. Military actions. Part 2

captivity	捕虜	horyo
to take captive	捕虜にする	horyo ni suru
to be in captivity	捕虜になる	horyo ni naru
to be taken prisoner	捕虜にされる	horyo ni sareru
concentration camp	強制収容所	kyōsei shūyō sho
prisoner of war	捕虜	horyo
to escape (vi)	逃げる	nigeru
to betray (vt)	裏切る	uragiru
betrayer	裏切り者	uragirimono

betrayal	裏切り	uragiri
to execute (shoot)	銃殺する	jūsatsu suru
execution (by firing squad)	銃殺刑	jūsatsu kei
equipment (military gear)	軍服	gunpuku
shoulder board	肩章	kenshō
gas mask	ガスマスク	gasumasuku
radio transmitter	軍用無線	gunyō musen
cipher, code	暗号	angō
secrecy	秘密	himitsu
password	パスワード	pasuwādo
land mine	地雷	jirai
to mine (road, etc.)	地雷を仕掛ける	jirai wo shikakeru
minefield	地雷原	jirai hara
air-raid warning	空襲警報	kūshū keihō
alarm (warning)	警報	keihō
signal	信号	shingō
signal flare	信号弾	shingō dan
headquarters	本部	honbu
reconnaissance	偵察	teisatsu
situation	事態	jitai
report	報告	hōkoku
ambush	奇襲	kishū
reinforcement (of army)	増援	zōen
target	標的	hyōteki
proving ground	実験場	jikken jō
military exercise	軍事演習	gunji enshū
panic	パニック	panikku
devastation	荒廃	kōhai
destruction, ruins	廃虚	haikyo
to destroy (vt)	廃虚にする	haikyo ni suru
to survive (vi, vt)	生き残る	ikinokoru
to disarm (vt)	武装解除する	busō kaijo suru
to handle (~ a gun)	扱う	atsukau
Attention!	気をつけ	ki wo tsuke
At ease!	休め	yasume
feat (of courage)	功績	kōseki
oath (vow)	誓い	chikai
to swear (an oath)	誓う	chikau
decoration (medal, etc.)	勲章	kunshō
to award (give medal to)	授ける	sazukeru
medal	メダル	medaru

order (e.g., ~ of Merit)	勲章	kunshō
victory	戦勝	senshō
defeat	敗北	haiboku
armistice	休戦	kyūsen
banner (standard)	旗	hata
glory (honor, fame)	栄光	eikō
parade	行進	kōshin
to march (on parade)	行進する	kōshin suru

114. Weapons

weapons	兵器	heiki
firearm	火器	kaki
cold weapons (knives, etc.)	冷兵器	reiheiki
chemical weapons	化学兵器	kagaku heiki
nuclear (adj)	核…	kaku …
nuclear weapons	核兵器	kakuheiki
bomb	爆弾	bakudan
atomic bomb	原子爆弾	genshi bakudan
pistol (gun)	拳銃、ピストル	kenjū, pisutoru
rifle	ライフル	raifuru
submachine gun	サブマシンガン	sabumashin gan
machine gun	マシンガン	mashin gan
muzzle	銃口	jūkō
barrel	砲身	hōshin
caliber	口径	kōkei
trigger	トリガー	torigā
sight (aiming device)	照準器	shōjun ki
magazine	弾倉	dansō
butt (of rifle)	台尻	daijiri
hand grenade	手榴弾	shuryūdan
explosive	爆発物	bakuhatsu butsu
bullet	弾	tama
cartridge	実弾	jitsudan
charge	装薬	sō yaku
ammunition	弾薬	danyaku
bomber (aircraft)	爆撃機	bakugeki ki
fighter	戦闘機	sentō ki
helicopter	ヘリコプター	herikoputā
anti-aircraft gun	対空砲	taikū hō

tank	戦車	sensha
tank gun	戦車砲	sensha hō
artillery	砲兵	hōhei
cannon	大砲	taihō
to lay (a gun)	狙いを定める	nerai wo sadameru
shell (projectile)	砲弾	hōdan
mortar bomb	迫撃砲弾	hakugeki hō dan
mortar	迫撃砲	hakugeki hō
splinter (shell fragment)	砲弾の破片	hōdan no hahen
submarine	潜水艦	sensui kan
torpedo	魚雷	gyorai
missile	ミサイル	misairu
to load (gun)	装填する	sōten suru
to shoot (vi)	撃つ	utsu
to point at (the cannon)	向ける	mukeru
bayonet	銃剣	jūken
epee	エペ	epe
saber (e.g., cavalry ~)	サーベル	sāberu
spear (weapon)	槍	yari
bow	弓	yumi
arrow	矢	ya
musket	マスケット銃	masuketto jū
crossbow	石弓	ishiyumi

115. Ancient people

primitive (prehistoric)	原始の	genshi no
prehistoric (adj)	先史時代の	senshi jidai no
ancient (~ civilization)	古代の	kodai no
Stone Age	石器時代	sekki jidai
Bronze Age	青銅器時代	seidōki jidai
Ice Age	氷河時代	hyōga jidai
tribe	部族	buzoku
cannibal	人食い人種	hito kui jin shi
hunter	狩人	karyūdo
to hunt (vi, vt)	狩る	karu
mammoth	マンモス	manmosu
cave	洞窟	dōkutsu
fire	火	hi
campfire	焚火	takibi
rock painting	岩壁画	iwa hekiga
tool (e.g., stone ax)	道具	dōgu

spear	槍	yari
stone ax	石斧	sekifu
to be at war	戦争中である	sensō chū de aru
to domesticate (vt)	飼い慣らす	kainarasu

idol	偶像	gūzō
to worship (vt)	崇拝する	sūhai suru
superstition	迷信	meishin
rite	儀式	gishiki

evolution	進化	shinka
development	発達	hattatsu
disappearance (extinction)	絶滅	zetsumetsu
to adapt oneself	適応する	tekiō suru

archeology	考古学	kōkogaku
archeologist	考古学者	kōkogakusha
archeological (adj)	考古学の	kōkogaku no

excavation site	発掘現場	hakkutsu genba
excavations	発掘	hakkutsu
find (object)	発見	hakken
fragment	一片	ippen

116. Middle Ages

people (ethnic group)	民族	minzoku
peoples	民族	minzoku
tribe	部族	buzoku
tribes	部族	buzoku

barbarians	野蛮人	yaban jin
Gauls	ガリア人	ga ria jin
Goths	ゴート人	gōto jin
Slavs	スラヴ人	suravu jin
Vikings	ヴァイキング	bai kingu

| Romans | ローマ人 | rōma jin |
| Roman (adj) | ローマの | rōma no |

Byzantines	ビザンティン人	bizantin jin
Byzantium	ビザンチウム	bizanchiumu
Byzantine (adj)	ビザンチンの	bizanchin no

emperor	皇帝	kōtei
leader, chief	リーダー	rīdā
powerful (~ king)	強力な	kyōryoku na
king	王	ō
ruler (sovereign)	支配者	shihai sha
knight	騎士	kishi

feudal lord	封建領主	hōken ryōshu
feudal (adj)	封建時代の	hōken jidai no
vassal	臣下	shinka
duke	公爵	kōshaku
earl	伯爵	hakushaku
baron	男爵	danshaku
bishop	司教	shikyō
armor	よろい [鎧]	yoroi
shield	盾	tate
sword	剣	ken
visor	バイザー	baizā
chainmail	鎖帷子	kusarikatabira
crusade	十字軍	jūjigun
crusader	十字軍の戦士	jūjigun no senshi
territory	領土	ryōdo
to attack (invade)	攻撃する	kōgeki suru
to conquer (vt)	征服する	seifuku suru
to occupy (invade)	占領する	senryō suru
siege (to be under ~)	包囲	hōi
besieged (adj)	攻囲された	kōi sare ta
to besiege (vt)	攻囲する	kōi suru
inquisition	宗教裁判	shūkyō saiban
inquisitor	宗教裁判官	shūkyō saibankan
torture	拷問	gōmon
cruel (adj)	残酷な	zankoku na
heretic	異端者	itan sha
heresy	異端	itan
seafaring	船旅	funatabi
pirate	海賊	kaizoku
piracy	海賊行為	kaizoku kōi
boarding (attack)	移乗攻撃	ijō kōgeki
loot, booty	戦利品	senri hin
treasures	宝	takara
discovery	発見	hakken
to discover (new land, etc.)	発見する	hakken suru
expedition	探検	tanken
musketeer	銃士	jū shi
cardinal	枢機卿	sūkikyō
heraldry	紋章学	monshō gaku
heraldic (adj)	紋章の	monshō no

117. Leader. Chief. Authorities

king	国王	kokuō
queen	女王	joō
royal (adj)	王室の	ōshitsu no
kingdom	王国	ōkoku
prince	王子	ōji
princess	王妃	ōhi
president	大統領	daitōryō
vice-president	副大統領	fuku daitōryō
senator	上院議員	jōin gīn
monarch	君主	kunshu
ruler (sovereign)	支配者	shihai sha
dictator	独裁者	dokusai sha
tyrant	暴君	bōkun
magnate	マグナート	magunāto
director	責任者	sekinin sha
chief	長	chō
manager (director)	管理者	kanri sha
boss	ボス	bosu
owner	経営者	keieisha
leader	リーダー	rīdā
head (~ of delegation)	長	chō
authorities	当局	tōkyoku
superiors	上司	jōshi
governor	知事	chiji
consul	領事	ryōji
diplomat	外交官	gaikō kan
mayor	市長	shichō
sheriff	保安官	hoan kan
emperor	皇帝	kōtei
tsar, czar	ツァーリ	tsāri
pharaoh	ファラオ	farao
khan	ハン	han

118. Breaking the law. Criminals. Part 1

bandit	山賊	sanzoku
crime	犯罪	hanzai
criminal (person)	犯罪者	hanzai sha
thief	泥棒	dorobō
to steal (vi, vt)	盗む	nusumu

stealing (larceny)	窃盗	settō
theft	泥棒	dorobō
to kidnap (vt)	誘拐する	yūkai suru
kidnapping	誘拐	yūkai
kidnapper	誘拐犯	yūkai han
ransom	身代金	minoshirokin
to demand ransom	身代金を要求する	minoshirokin wo yōkyū suru
to rob (vt)	強盗する	gōtō suru
robbery	強盗	gōtō
robber	強盗犯	gōtō han
to extort (vt)	恐喝する	kyōkatsu suru
extortionist	恐喝者	kyōkatsu sha
extortion	恐喝	kyōkatsu
to murder, to kill	殺す	korosu
murder	殺人	satsujin
murderer	殺人者	satsujin sha
gunshot	発砲	happō
to fire a shot	発砲する	happō suru
to shoot to death	射殺する	shasatsu suru
to shoot (vi)	撃つ	utsu
shooting	射撃	shageki
incident (fight, etc.)	事件	jiken
fight, brawl	喧嘩	kenka
Help!	助けて！	tasuke te!
victim	被害者	higai sha
to damage (vt)	損害を与える	songai wo ataeru
damage	損害	songai
dead body	死体	shitai
grave (~ crime)	重い	omoi
to attack (vt)	攻撃する	kōgeki suru
to beat (dog, person)	殴る	naguru
to beat up	打ちのめす	uchinomesu
to take (rob of sth)	強奪する	gōdatsu suru
to stab to death	刺し殺す	sashikorosu
to maim (vt)	重症を負わせる	jūshō wo owaseru
to wound (vt)	負わせる	owaseru
blackmail	恐喝	kyōkatsu
to blackmail (vt)	恐喝する	kyōkatsu suru
blackmailer	恐喝者	kyōkatsu sha
protection racket	ゆすり	yusuri
racketeer	ゆすりを働く人	yusuri wo hataraku hito

| gangster | 暴力団員 | bōryokudan in |
| mafia, Mob | マフィア | mafia |

pickpocket	すり	suri
burglar	強盗	gōtō
smuggling	密輸	mitsuyu
smuggler	密輸者	mitsuyu sha

forgery	偽造	gizō
to forge (counterfeit)	偽造する	gizō suru
fake (forged)	偽造の	gizō no

119. Breaking the law. Criminals. Part 2

rape	強姦	gōkan
to rape (vt)	強姦する	gōkan suru
rapist	強姦犯	gōkan han
maniac	マニア	mania

prostitute (fem.)	売春婦	baishun fu
prostitution	売春	baishun
pimp	ポン引き	pon biki

| drug addict | 麻薬中毒者 | mayaku chūdoku sha |
| drug dealer | 麻薬の売人 | mayaku no bainin |

to blow up (bomb)	爆発させる	bakuhatsu saseru
explosion	爆発	bakuhatsu
to set fire	放火する	hōka suru
incendiary (arsonist)	放火犯人	hōka hannin

terrorism	テロリズム	terorizumu
terrorist	テロリスト	terorisuto
hostage	人質	hitojichi

to swindle (vt)	詐欺を働く	sagi wo hataraku
swindle	詐欺	sagi
swindler	詐欺師	sagi shi

to bribe (vt)	賄賂を渡す	wairo wo watasu
bribery	賄賂の授受	wairo no juju
bribe	賄賂	wairo

poison	毒	doku
to poison (vt)	…を毒殺する	… wo dokusatsu suru
to poison oneself	毒薬を飲む	dokuyaku wo nomu

suicide (act)	自殺	jisatsu
suicide (person)	自殺者	jisatsu sha
to threaten (vt)	脅す	odosu

threat	脅し	odoshi
to make an attempt	殺そうとする	koroso u to suru
attempt (attack)	殺人未遂	satsujin misui
to steal (a car)	盗む	nusumu
to hijack (a plane)	ハイジャックする	haijakku suru
revenge	復讐	fukushū
to revenge (vt)	復讐する	fukushū suru
to torture (vt)	拷問する	gōmon suru
torture	拷問	gōmon
to torment (vt)	虐待する	gyakutai suru
pirate	海賊	kaizoku
hooligan	フーリガン	fūrigan
armed (adj)	武装した	busō shi ta
violence	暴力	bōryoku
illegal (unlawful)	違法な	ihō na
spying (n)	スパイ行為	supai kōi
to spy (vi)	スパイする	supai suru

120. Police. Law. Part 1

justice	司法	shihō
court (court room)	裁判所	saibansho
judge	裁判官	saibankan
jurors	陪審員	baishin in
jury trial	陪審裁判	baishin saiban
to judge (vt)	判決を下す	hanketsu wo kudasu
lawyer, attorney	弁護士	bengoshi
accused	被告人	hikoku jin
dock	被告席	hikoku seki
charge	告発	kokuhatsu
accused	被告人	hikoku jin
sentence	判決	hanketsu
to sentence (vt)	判決を下す	hanketsu wo kudasu
guilty (culprit)	有罪の	yūzai no
to punish (vt)	処罰する	shobatsu suru
punishment	処罰	shobatsu
fine (penalty)	罰金	bakkin
life imprisonment	終身刑	shūshin kei
death penalty	死刑	shikei

electric chair	電気椅子	denki isu
gallows	絞首台	kōshu dai
to execute (vt)	処刑する	shokei suru
execution	死刑	shikei
prison, jail	刑務所	keimusho
cell	独房	dokubō
escort	護送	gosō
prison guard	刑務官	keimu kan
prisoner	囚人	shūjin
handcuffs	手錠	tejō
to handcuff (vt)	手錠をかける	tejō wo kakeru
prison break	脱獄	datsugoku
to break out (vi)	脱獄する	datsugoku suru
to disappear (vi)	姿を消す	sugata wo kesu
to release (from prison)	放免する	hōmen suru
amnesty	恩赦	onsha
police	警察	keisatsu
police officer	警官	keikan
police station	警察署	keisatsu sho
billy club	警棒	keibō
bullhorn	拡声器	kakusei ki
patrol car	パトロールカー	patorōrukā
siren	サイレン	sairen
to turn on the siren	サイレンを鳴らす	sairen wo narasu
siren call	サイレンの音	sairen no oto
crime scene	犯行現場	hankō genba
witness	目撃者	mokugeki sha
freedom	自由	jiyū
accomplice	共犯者	kyōhan sha
to flee (vi)	逃走する	tōsō suru
trace (to leave a ~)	形跡	keiseki

121. Police. Law. Part 2

search (investigation)	捜査	sōsa
to look for ...	捜索する	sōsaku suru
suspicion	嫌疑	kengi
suspicious (suspect)	不審な	fushin na
to stop (cause to halt)	止める	tomeru
to detain (keep in custody)	留置する	ryūchi suru
case (lawsuit)	事件	jiken
investigation	捜査	sōsa

detective	探偵	tantei
investigator	捜査官	sōsa kan
hypothesis	仮説	kasetsu

motive	動機	dōki
interrogation	尋問	jinmon
to interrogate (vt)	尋問する	jinmon suru
to question (vt)	尋問する	jinmon suru
check (identity ~)	身元確認	mimoto kakunin

round-up	一斉検挙	issei kenkyo
search (~ warrant)	家宅捜索	kataku sōsaku
chase (pursuit)	追跡	tsuiseki
to pursue, to chase	追跡する	tsuiseki suru
to track (a criminal)	追う	ō

arrest	逮捕	taiho
to arrest (sb)	逮捕する	taiho suru
to catch (thief, etc.)	捕まえる	tsukamaeru
capture	捕獲	hokaku

document	文書	bunsho
proof (evidence)	証拠	shōko
to prove (vt)	証明する	shōmei suru
footprint	足跡	ashiato
fingerprints	指紋	shimon
piece of evidence	一つの証拠	hitotsu no shōko

alibi	アリバイ	aribai
innocent (not guilty)	無罪の	muzai no
injustice	不当	futō
unjust, unfair (adj)	不当な	futō na

criminal (adj)	犯罪の	hanzai no
to confiscate (vt)	没収する	bosshū suru
drug (illegal substance)	麻薬	mayaku
weapon, gun	兵器	heiki
to disarm (vt)	武装解除する	busō kaijo suru
to order (command)	命令する	meirei suru
to disappear (vi)	姿を消す	sugata wo kesu

law	法律	hōritsu
legal, lawful (adj)	合法の	gōhō no
illegal, illicit (adj)	違法な	ihō na

| responsibility (blame) | 責め | seme |
| responsible (adj) | 責めを負うべき | seme wo ō beki |

NATURE

The Earth. Part 1

122. Outer space

cosmos	宇宙	uchū
space (as adj)	宇宙の	uchū no
outer space	宇宙空間	uchū kūkan
world	世界	sekai
universe	宇宙	uchū
galaxy	銀河系	gingakei
star	星	hoshi
constellation	星座	seiza
planet	惑星	wakusei
satellite	衛星	eisei
meteorite	隕石	inseki
comet	彗星	suisei
asteroid	小惑星	shōwakusei
orbit	軌道	kidō
to revolve (~ around the Earth)	公転する	kōten suru
atmosphere	大気	taiki
the Sun	太陽	taiyō
solar system	太陽系	taiyōkei
solar eclipse	日食	nisshoku
the Earth	地球	chikyū
the Moon	月	tsuki
Mars	火星	kasei
Venus	金星	kinsei
Jupiter	木星	mokusei
Saturn	土星	dosei
Mercury	水星	suisei
Uranus	天王星	tennōsei
Neptune	海王星	kaiōsei
Pluto	冥王星	meiōsei
Milky Way	天の川	amanogawa
Great Bear	おおぐま座	ōguma za

North Star	北極星	hokkyokusei
Martian	火星人	kasei jin
extraterrestrial (n)	宇宙人	uchū jin
alien	異星人	i hoshi jin
flying saucer	空飛ぶ円盤	sora tobu enban
spaceship	宇宙船	uchūsen
space station	宇宙ステーション	uchū sutēshon
blast-off	打ち上げ	uchiage
engine	エンジン	enjin
nozzle	ノズル	nozuru
fuel	燃料	nenryō
cockpit, flight deck	コックピット	kokkupitto
antenna	アンテナ	antena
porthole	舷窓	gensō
solar battery	太陽電池	taiyō denchi
spacesuit	宇宙服	uchū fuku
weightlessness	無重力	mu jūryoku
oxygen	酸素	sanso
docking (in space)	ドッキング	dokkingu
to dock (vi, vt)	ドッキングする	dokkingu suru
observatory	天文台	tenmondai
telescope	望遠鏡	bōenkyō
to observe (vt)	観察する	kansatsu suru
to explore (vt)	探索する	tansaku suru

123. The Earth

the Earth	地球	chikyū
globe (the Earth)	世界	sekai
planet	惑星	wakusei
atmosphere	大気	taiki
geography	地理学	chiri gaku
nature	自然	shizen
globe (table ~)	地球儀	chikyūgi
map	地図	chizu
atlas	地図帳	chizu chō
Europe	ヨーロッパ	yōroppa
Asia	アジア	ajia
Africa	アフリカ	afurika
Australia	オーストラリア	ōsutoraria
America	アメリカ	amerika

| North America | 北アメリカ | kita amerika |
| South America | 南アメリカ | minami amerika |

| Antarctica | 南極大陸 | nankyokutairiku |
| the Arctic | 北極 | hokkyoku |

124. Cardinal directions

north	北	kita
to the north	北へ	kita he
in the north	北に	kita ni
northern (adj)	北の	kita no

south	南	minami
to the south	南へ	minami he
in the south	南に	minami ni
southern (adj)	南の	minami no

west	西	nishi
to the west	西へ	nishi he
in the west	西に	nishi ni
western (adj)	西の	nishi no

east	東	higashi
to the east	東へ	higashi he
in the east	東に	higashi ni
eastern (adj)	東の	higashi no

125. Sea. Ocean

sea	海	umi
ocean	海洋	kaiyō
gulf (bay)	湾	wan
straits	海峡	kaikyō

solid ground	乾燥地	kansō chi
continent (mainland)	大陸	tairiku
island	島	shima
peninsula	半島	hantō
archipelago	多島海	tatōkai

bay, cove	入り江	irie
harbor	泊地	hakuchi
lagoon	潟	kata
cape	岬	misaki

| atoll | 環礁 | kanshō |
| reef | 暗礁 | anshō |

coral	サンゴ	sango
coral reef	サンゴ礁	sangoshō
deep (adj)	深い	fukai
depth (deep water)	深さ	fuka sa
abyss	深淵	shinen
trench (e.g., Mariana ~)	海溝	kaikō
current, stream	海流	kairyū
to surround (bathe)	取り囲む	torikakomu
shore	海岸	kaigan
coast	沿岸	engan
high tide	満潮	manchō
low tide	干潮	kanchō
sandbank	砂州	sasu
bottom	底	soko
wave	波	nami
crest (~ of a wave)	波頭	namigashira
froth (foam)	泡	awa
storm	嵐	arashi
hurricane	ハリケーン	harikēn
tsunami	津波	tsunami
calm (dead ~)	凪	nagi
quiet, calm (adj)	穏やかな	odayaka na
pole	極地	kyokuchi
polar (adj)	極地の	kyokuchi no
latitude	緯度	ido
longitude	経度	keido
parallel	度線	dosen
equator	赤道	sekidō
sky	空	sora
horizon	地平線	chiheisen
air	空気	kūki
lighthouse	灯台	tōdai
to dive (vi)	飛び込む	tobikomu
to sink (ab. boat)	沈没する	chinbotsu suru
treasures	宝	takara

126. Seas' and Oceans' names

Atlantic Ocean	大西洋	taiseiyō
Indian Ocean	インド洋	indoyō

Pacific Ocean	太平洋	taiheiyō
Arctic Ocean	北氷洋	kitakōriyō
Black Sea	黒海	kokkai
Red Sea	紅海	kōkai
Yellow Sea	黄海	kōkai
White Sea	白海	hakkai
Caspian Sea	カスピ海	kasupikai
Dead Sea	死海	shikai
Mediterranean Sea	地中海	chichūkai
Aegean Sea	エーゲ海	ēgekai
Adriatic Sea	アドリア海	adoriakai
Arabian Sea	アラビア海	arabia kai
Sea of Japan	日本海	nihonkai
Bering Sea	ベーリング海	bēringukai
South China Sea	南シナ海	minami shinakai
Coral Sea	珊瑚海	sangokai
Tasman Sea	タスマン海	tasumankai
Caribbean Sea	カリブ海	karibukai
Barents Sea	バレンツ海	barentsukai
Kara Sea	カラ海	karakai
North Sea	北海	hokkai
Baltic Sea	バルト海	barutokai
Norwegian Sea	ノルウェー海	noruwē umi

127. Mountains

mountain	山	yama
mountain range	山脈	sanmyaku
mountain ridge	山稜	sanryō
summit, top	頂上	chōjō
peak	とがった山頂	togatta sanchō
foot (of mountain)	麓	fumoto
slope (mountainside)	山腹	sanpuku
volcano	火山	kazan
active volcano	活火山	kakkazan
dormant volcano	休火山	kyūkazan
eruption	噴火	funka
crater	噴火口	funkakō
magma	岩漿、マグマ	ganshō, maguma
lava	溶岩	yōgan

molten (~ lava)	溶…	yō …
canyon	峡谷	kyōkoku
gorge	峡谷	kyōkoku
crevice	裂け目	sakeme
abyss (chasm)	奈落の底	naraku no soko

pass, col	峠	tōge
plateau	高原	kōgen
cliff	断崖	dangai
hill	丘	oka

glacier	氷河	hyōga
waterfall	滝	taki
geyser	間欠泉	kanketsusen
lake	湖	mizūmi

plain	平原	heigen
landscape	風景	fūkei
echo	こだま	kodama

alpinist	登山家	tozan ka
rock climber	ロッククライマー	rokku kuraimā
to conquer (in climbing)	征服する	seifuku suru
climb (an easy ~)	登山	tozan

128. Mountains names

Alps	アルプス山脈	arupusu sanmyaku
Mont Blanc	モンブラン	monburan
Pyrenees	ピレネー山脈	pirenē sanmyaku

Carpathians	カルパティア山脈	karupatia sanmyaku
Ural Mountains	ウラル山脈	uraru sanmyaku
Caucasus	コーカサス山脈	kōkasasu sanmyaku
Elbrus	エルブルス山	eruburusu san

Altai	アルタイ山脈	arutai sanmyaku
Tien Shan	天山山脈	amayama sanmyaku
Pamir Mountains	パミール高原	pamīru kōgen
Himalayas	ヒマラヤ	himaraya
Everest	エベレスト	eberesuto
Andes	アンデス山脈	andesu sanmyaku
Kilimanjaro	キリマンジャロ	kirimanjaro

129. Rivers

| river | 川 | kawa |
| spring (natural source) | 泉 | izumi |

riverbed	川床	kawadoko
basin	流域	ryūiki
to flow into ...	...に流れ込む	... ni nagarekomu
tributary	支流	shiryū
bank (of river)	川岸	kawagishi
current, stream	流れ	nagare
downstream (adv)	下流の	karyū no
upstream (adv)	上流の	jōryū no
inundation	洪水	kōzui
flooding	氾濫	hanran
to overflow (vi)	氾濫する	hanran suru
to flood (vt)	水浸しにする	mizubitashi ni suru
shallows (shoal)	浅瀬	asase
rapids	急流	kyūryū
dam	ダム	damu
canal	運河	unga
artificial lake	ため池 [溜池]	tameike
sluice, lock	水門	suimon
water body (pond, etc.)	水域	suīki
swamp, bog	沼地	numachi
marsh	湿地	shicchi
whirlpool	渦	uzu
stream (brook)	小川	ogawa
drinking (ab. water)	飲用の	inyō no
fresh (~ water)	淡...	tan ...
ice	氷	kōri
to freeze (ab. river, etc.)	氷結する	hyōketsu suru

130. Rivers' names

Seine	セーヌ川	sēnu gawa
Loire	ロワール川	rowāru gawa
Thames	テムズ川	temuzu gawa
Rhine	ライン川	rain gawa
Danube	ドナウ川	donau gawa
Volga	ヴォルガ川	voruga gawa
Don	ドン川	don gawa
Lena	レナ川	rena gawa
Yellow River	黄河	kōga
Yangtze	長江	chōkō

Mekong	メコン川	mekon gawa
Ganges	ガンジス川	ganjisu gawa
Nile River	ナイル川	nairu gawa
Congo	コンゴ川	kongo gawa
Okavango	オカヴァンゴ川	okavango gawa
Zambezi	ザンベジ川	zanbeji gawa
Limpopo	リンポポ川	rinpopo gawa
Mississippi River	ミシシッピ川	mishishippi gawa

131. Forest

forest	森林	shinrin
forest (as adj)	森林の	shinrin no
thick forest	密林	mitsurin
grove	木立	kodachi
forest clearing	空き地	akichi
thicket	やぶ [藪]	yabu
scrubland	低木地域	teiboku chīki
footpath (troddenpath)	小道	komichi
gully	ガリ	gari
tree	木	ki
leaf	葉	ha
leaves	葉っぱ	happa
fall of leaves	落葉	rakuyō
to fall (ab. leaves)	落ちる	ochiru
top (of the tree)	木のてっぺん	kinoteppen
branch	枝	eda
bough	主枝	shushi
bud (on shrub, tree)	芽 [め]	me
needle (of pine tree)	松葉	matsuba
pine cone	松ぼっくり	matsubokkuri
hollow (in a tree)	樹洞	kihora
nest	巣	su
burrow (animal hole)	巣穴	su ana
trunk	幹	miki
root	根	ne
bark	樹皮	juhi
moss	コケ [苔]	koke
to uproot (vt)	根こそぎにする	nekosogi ni suru
to chop down	切り倒す	kiritaosu

to deforest (vt)	切り払う	kiriharau
tree stump	切り株	kirikabu
campfire	焚火	takibi
forest fire	森林火災	shinrin kasai
to extinguish (vt)	火を消す	hi wo kesu
forest ranger	森林警備隊員	shinrin keibi taīn
protection	保護	hogo
to protect (~ nature)	保護する	hogo suru
poacher	密漁者	mitsuryō sha
trap (e.g., bear ~)	罠	wana
to pick (mushrooms)	摘み集める	tsumi atsumeru
to pick (berries)	採る	toru
to lose one's way	道に迷う	michi ni mayō

132. Natural resources

natural resources	天然資源	tennen shigen
minerals	鉱物資源	kōbutsu shigen
deposits	鉱床	kōshō
field (e.g., oilfield)	田	den
to mine (extract)	採掘する	saikutsu suru
mining (extraction)	採掘	saikutsu
ore	鉱石	kōseki
mine (e.g., for coal)	鉱山	kōzan
mine shaft, pit	立坑	tatekō
miner	鉱山労働者	kōzan rōdō sha
gas	ガス	gasu
gas pipeline	ガスパイプライン	gasu paipurain
oil (petroleum)	石油	sekiyu
oil pipeline	石油パイプライン	sekiyu paipurain
oil well	油井	yusei
derrick	油井やぐら	yusei ya gura
tanker	タンカー	tankā
sand	砂	suna
limestone	石灰岩	sekkaigan
gravel	砂利	jari
peat	泥炭	deitan
clay	粘土	nendo
coal	石炭	sekitan
iron	鉄	tetsu
gold	金	kin
silver	銀	gin

nickel	ニッケル	nikkeru
copper	銅	dō
zinc	亜鉛	aen
manganese	マンガン	mangan
mercury	水銀	suigin
lead	鉛	namari
mineral	鉱物	kōbutsu
crystal	水晶	suishō
marble	大理石	dairiseki
uranium	ウラン	uran

The Earth. Part 2

133. Weather

weather	天気	tenki
weather forecast	天気予報	tenki yohō
temperature	温度	ondo
thermometer	温度計	ondo kei
barometer	気圧計	kiatsu kei
humid (adj)	湿度の	shitsudo no
humidity	湿度	shitsudo
heat (extreme ~)	猛暑	mōsho
hot (torrid)	暑い	atsui
it's hot	暑いです	atsui desu
it's warm	暖かいです	atatakai desu
warm (moderately hot)	暖かい	atatakai
it's cold	寒いです	samui desu
cold (adj)	寒い	samui
sun	太陽	taiyō
to shine (vi)	照る	teru
sunny (day)	晴れの	hare no
to come up (vi)	昇る	noboru
to set (vi)	沈む	shizumu
cloud	雲	kumo
cloudy (adj)	曇りの	kumori no
rain cloud	雨雲	amagumo
somber (gloomy)	どんよりした	donyori shi ta
rain	雨	ame
it's raining	雨が降っている	ame ga futte iru
rainy (day)	雨の	ame no
to drizzle (vi)	そぼ降る	sobofuru
pouring rain	土砂降りの雨	doshaburi no ame
downpour	大雨	ōame
heavy (e.g., ~ rain)	激しい	hageshī
puddle	水溜り	mizutamari
to get wet (in rain)	ぬれる [濡れる]	nureru
fog (mist)	霧	kiri
foggy	霧の	kiri no

| snow | 雪 | yuki |
| it's snowing | 雪が降っている | yuki ga futte iru |

134. Severe weather. Natural disasters

thunderstorm	雷雨	raiu
lightning (~ strike)	稲妻	inazuma
to flash (vi)	ピカッと光る	pikatto hikaru

thunder	雷	kaminari
to thunder (vi)	雷が鳴る	kaminari ga naru
it's thundering	雷が鳴っている	kaminari ga natte iru

| hail | ひょう [雹] | hyō |
| it's hailing | ひょうが降っている | hyō ga futte iru |

| to flood (vt) | 水浸しにする | mizubitashi ni suru |
| flood, inundation | 洪水 | kōzui |

earthquake	地震	jishin
tremor, quake	震動	shindō
epicenter	震源地	shingen chi

| eruption | 噴火 | funka |
| lava | 溶岩 | yōgan |

twister	旋風	senpū
tornado	竜巻	tatsumaki
typhoon	台風	taifū

hurricane	ハリケーン	harikēn
storm	暴風	bōfū
tsunami	津波	tsunami

cyclone	サイクロン	saikuron
bad weather	悪い天気	warui tenki
fire (accident)	火事	kaji
disaster	災害	saigai
meteorite	隕石	inseki

avalanche	雪崩	nadare
snowslide	雪崩	nadare
blizzard	猛吹雪	mō fubuki
snowstorm	吹雪	fubuki

Fauna

135. Mammals. Predators

predator	肉食獣	nikushoku juu
tiger	トラ [虎]	tora
lion	ライオン	raion
wolf	オオカミ	ōkami
fox	キツネ [狐]	kitsune
jaguar	ジャガー	jagā
leopard	ヒョウ [豹]	hyō
cheetah	チーター	chītā
black panther	黒豹	kuro hyō
puma	ピューマ	pyūma
snow leopard	雪豹	yuki hyō
lynx	オオヤマネコ	ōyamaneko
coyote	コヨーテ	koyōte
jackal	ジャッカル	jakkaru
hyena	ハイエナ	haiena

136. Wild animals

animal	動物	dōbutsu
beast (animal)	獣	shishi
squirrel	リス	risu
hedgehog	ハリネズミ [針鼠]	harinezumi
hare	ヘア	hea
rabbit	ウサギ [兎]	usagi
badger	アナグマ	anaguma
raccoon	アライグマ	araiguma
hamster	ハムスター	hamusutā
marmot	マーモット	māmotto
mole	モグラ	mogura
mouse	ネズミ	nezumi
rat	ラット	ratto
bat	コウモリ [蝙蝠]	kōmori
ermine	オコジョ	okojo
sable	クロテン	kuroten

marten	マツテン	matsu ten
weasel	イタチ (鼬、鼬鼠)	itachi
mink	ミンク	minku

| beaver | ビーバー | bībā |
| otter | カワウソ | kawauso |

horse	ウマ [馬]	uma
moose	ヘラジカ (箆鹿)	herajika
deer	シカ [鹿]	shika
camel	ラクダ [駱駝]	rakuda

bison	アメリカバイソン	amerika baison
aurochs	ヨーロッパバイソン	yōroppa baison
buffalo	水牛	suigyū

zebra	シマウマ [縞馬]	shimauma
antelope	レイヨウ	reiyō
roe deer	ノロジカ	noro jika
fallow deer	ダマジカ	damajika
chamois	シャモア	shamoa
wild boar	イノシシ [猪]	inoshishi

whale	クジラ [鯨]	kujira
seal	アザラシ	azarashi
walrus	セイウチ [海象]	seiuchi
fur seal	オットセイ [膃肭臍]	ottosei
dolphin	いるか [海豚]	iruka

bear	クマ [熊]	kuma
polar bear	ホッキョクグマ	hokkyokuguma
panda	パンダ	panda

monkey	サル [猿]	saru
chimpanzee	チンパンジー	chinpanjī
orangutan	オランウータン	oranwutan
gorilla	ゴリラ	gorira
macaque	マカク	makaku
gibbon	テナガザル	tenagazaru

elephant	ゾウ [象]	zō
rhinoceros	サイ [犀]	sai
giraffe	キリン	kirin
hippopotamus	カバ [河馬]	kaba

| kangaroo | カンガルー | kangarū |
| koala (bear) | コアラ | koara |

mongoose	マングース	mangūsu
chinchilla	チンチラ	chinchira
skunk	スカンク	sukanku
porcupine	ヤマアラシ	yamārashi

137. Domestic animals

cat	猫	neko
tomcat	オス猫	osu neko
dog	犬	inu
horse	ウマ［馬］	uma
stallion	種馬	taneuma
mare	雌馬	meuma
cow	雌牛	meushi
bull	雄牛	ōshi
ox	去勢牛	kyosei ushi
sheep	羊	hitsuji
ram	雄羊	ohitsuji
goat	ヤギ［山羊］	yagi
billy goat, he-goat	雄ヤギ	oyagi
donkey	ロバ	roba
mule	ラバ	raba
pig	ブタ［豚］	buta
piglet	子豚	kobuta
rabbit	カイウサギ［飼兎］	kai usagi
hen (chicken)	ニワトリ［鶏］	niwatori
rooster	おんどり［雄鶏］	ondori
duck	アヒル	ahiru
drake	雄アヒル	oahiru
goose	ガチョウ	gachō
tom turkey	雄七面鳥	oshichimenchō
turkey (hen)	七面鳥［シチメンチョウ］	shichimenchō
domestic animals	家畜	kachiku
tame (e.g., ~ hamster)	馴れた	nare ta
to tame (vt)	かいならす	kainarasu
to breed (vt)	飼養する	shiyō suru
farm	農場	nōjō
poultry	家禽	kakin
cattle	畜牛	chiku gyū
herd (cattle)	群れ	mure
stable	馬小屋	umagoya
pigsty	豚小屋	buta goya
cowshed	牛舎	gyūsha
rabbit hutch	ウサギ小屋	usagi koya
hen house	鶏小屋	niwatori goya

138. Birds

bird	鳥	tori
pigeon	鳩 [ハト]	hato
sparrow	スズメ (雀)	suzume
tit	シジュウカラ [四十雀]	shijūkara
magpie	カササギ (鵲)	kasasagi
raven	ワタリガラス [渡鴉]	watari garasu
crow	カラス [鴉]	karasu
jackdaw	ニシコクマルガラス	nishikokumaru garasu
rook	ミヤマガラス [深山鳥]	miyama garasu
duck	カモ [鴨]	kamo
goose	ガチョウ	gachō
pheasant	キジ	kiji
eagle	鷲	washi
hawk	鷹	taka
falcon	ハヤブサ [隼]	hayabusa
vulture	ハゲワシ	hagewashi
condor (Andean ~)	コンドル	kondoru
swan	白鳥 [ハクチョウ]	hakuchō
crane	鶴 [ツル]	tsuru
stork	シュバシコウ	shubashikō
parrot	オウム	ōmu
hummingbird	ハチドリ [蜂鳥]	hachidori
peacock	クジャク [孔雀]	kujaku
ostrich	ダチョウ [駝鳥]	dachō
heron	サギ [鷺]	sagi
flamingo	フラミンゴ	furamingo
pelican	ペリカン	perikan
nightingale	サヨナキドリ	sayonakidori
swallow	ツバメ [燕]	tsubame
thrush	ノハラツグミ	nohara tsugumi
song thrush	ウタツグミ [歌鶫]	uta tsugumi
blackbird	クロウタドリ	kurōtadori
swift	アマツバメ [雨燕]	ama tsubame
lark	ヒバリ [雲雀]	hibari
quail	ウズラ	uzura
woodpecker	キツツキ	kitsutsuki
cuckoo	カッコウ [郭公]	kakkō
owl	トラフズク	torafuzuku
eagle owl	ワシミミズク	washi mimizuku

wood grouse	ヨーロッパ オオライチョウ	yōroppa ōraichō
black grouse	クロライチョウ	kuro raichō
partridge	ヨーロッパヤマウズラ	yōroppa yamauzura
starling	ムクドリ	mukudori
canary	カナリア [金糸雀]	kanaria
hazel grouse	エゾライチョウ	ezo raichō
chaffinch	ズアオアトリ	zuaoatori
bullfinch	ウソ [鷽]	uso
seagull	カモメ [鷗]	kamome
albatross	アホウドリ	ahōdori
penguin	ペンギン	pengin

139. Fish. Marine animals

bream	ブリーム	burīmu
carp	コイ [鯉]	koi
perch	ヨーロピアンパーチ	yōropian pāchi
catfish	ナマズ	namazu
pike	カワカマス	kawakamasu
salmon	サケ	sake
sturgeon	チョウザメ [蝶鮫]	chōzame
herring	ニシン	nishin
Atlantic salmon	タイセイヨウサケ [大西洋鮭]	taiseiyō sake
mackerel	サバ [鯖]	saba
flatfish	カレイ [鰈]	karei
zander, pike perch	ザンダー	zandā
cod	タラ [鱈]	tara
tuna	マグロ [鮪]	maguro
trout	マス [鱒]	masu
eel	ウナギ [鰻]	unagi
electric ray	シビレエイ	shibireei
moray eel	ウツボ [鱓]	utsubo
piranha	ピラニア	pirania
shark	サメ [鮫]	same
dolphin	イルカ [海豚]	iruka
whale	クジラ [鯨]	kujira
crab	カニ [蟹]	kani
jellyfish	クラゲ [水母]	kurage
octopus	タコ [蛸]	tako
starfish	ヒトデ [海星]	hitode

sea urchin	ウニ [海胆]	uni
seahorse	タツノオトシゴ	tatsunootoshigo
oyster	カキ [牡蠣]	kaki
shrimp	エビ	ebi
lobster	イセエビ	iseebi
spiny lobster	スパイニーロブスター	supainī robusutā

140. Amphibians. Reptiles

snake	ヘビ（蛇）	hebi
venomous (snake)	毒…、 有毒な	doku…, yūdoku na
viper	クサリヘビ	kusarihebi
cobra	コブラ	kobura
python	ニシキヘビ	nishikihebi
boa	ボア	boa
grass snake	ヨーロッパヤマカガシ	yōroppa yamakagashi
rattle snake	ガラガラヘビ	garagarahebi
anaconda	アナコンダ	anakonda
lizard	トカゲ [蜥蜴]	tokage
iguana	イグアナ	iguana
monitor lizard	オオトカゲ	ōtokage
salamander	サンショウウオ [山椒魚]	sanshōuo
chameleon	カメレオン	kamereon
scorpion	サソリ [蠍]	sasori
turtle	カメ [亀]	kame
frog	蛙 [カエル]	kaeru
toad	ヒキガエル	hikigaeru
crocodile	ワニ [鰐]	wani

141. Insects

insect, bug	昆虫	konchū
butterfly	チョウ [蝶]	chō
ant	アリ [蟻]	ari
fly	ハエ [蝿]	hae
mosquito	カ [蚊]	ka
beetle	甲虫	kabutomushi
wasp	ワスプ	wasupu
bee	ハチ [蜂]	hachi
bumblebee	マルハナバチ [丸花蜂]	maruhanabachi
gadfly	アブ [虻]	abu
spider	クモ [蜘蛛]	kumo

spider's web	クモの巣	kumo no su
dragonfly	トンボ [蜻蛉]	tonbo
grasshopper	キリギリス	kirigirisu
moth (night butterfly)	ガ [蛾]	ga

cockroach	ゴキブリ [蜚蠊]	gokiburi
tick	ダニ [壁蝨、蜱]	dani
flea	ノミ [蚤]	nomi
midge	ヌカカ [糠蚊]	nukaka

locust	バッタ [飛蝗]	batta
snail	カタツムリ [蝸牛]	katatsumuri
cricket	コオロギ [蟋蟀、蛬]	kōrogi
lightning bug	ホタル [蛍、螢]	hotaru
ladybug	テントウムシ [天道虫]	tentōmushi
cockchafer	コフキコガネ	kofukikogane

leech	ヒル [蛭]	hiru
caterpillar	ケムシ [毛虫]	kemushi
earthworm	ミミズ [蚯蚓]	mimizu
larva	幼虫	yōchū

Flora

142. Trees

tree	木	ki
deciduous (adj)	落葉性の	rakuyō sei no
coniferous (adj)	針葉樹の	shinyōju no
evergreen (adj)	常緑の	jōryoku no
apple tree	りんごの木	ringonoki
pear tree	洋梨の木	yōnashinoki
sweet cherry tree	セイヨウミザクラ	seiyōmi zakura
sour cherry tree	スミミザクラ	sumimi zakura
plum tree	プラムトリー	puramu torī
birch	カバノキ	kabanoki
oak	オーク	ōku
linden tree	シナノキ [科の木]	shinanoki
aspen	ヤマナラシ [山鳴らし]	yamanarashi
maple	カエデ [楓]	kaede
spruce	スプルース	supurūsu
pine	マツ [松]	matsu
larch	カラマツ [唐松]	karamatsu
fir tree	モミ [樅]	momi
cedar	シダー	shidā
poplar	ポプラ	popura
rowan	ナナカマド	nanakamado
willow	ヤナギ [柳]	yanagi
alder	ハンノキ	hannoki
beech	ブナ	buna
elm	ニレ [楡]	nire
ash (tree)	トネリコ [梣]	toneriko
chestnut	クリ [栗]	kuri
magnolia	モクレン [木蓮]	mokuren
palm tree	ヤシ [椰子]	yashi
cypress	イトスギ [糸杉]	itosugi
mangrove	マングローブ	mangurōbu
baobab	バオバブ	baobabu
eucalyptus	ユーカリ	yūkari
sequoia	セコイア	sekoia

143. Shrubs

bush	低木	teiboku
shrub	潅木	kanboku
grapevine	ブドウ [葡萄]	budō
vineyard	ブドウ園 [葡萄園]	budōen
raspberry bush	ラズベリー	razuberī
blackcurrant bush	クロスグリ	kuro suguri
redcurrant bush	フサスグリ	fusa suguri
gooseberry bush	セイヨウスグリ	seiyō suguri
acacia	アカシア	akashia
barberry	メギ	megi
jasmine	ジャスミン	jasumin
juniper	セイヨウネズ	seiyōnezu
rosebush	バラの木	baranoki
dog rose	イヌバラ	inu bara

144. Fruits. Berries

fruit	果物	kudamono
fruits	果物	kudamono
apple	リンゴ	ringo
pear	洋梨	yōnashi
plum	プラム	puramu
strawberry	イチゴ（苺）	ichigo
cherry	チェリー	cherī
sour cherry	サワー チェリー	sawā cherī
sweet cherry	スイート チェリー	suīto cherī
grape	ブドウ [葡萄]	budō
raspberry	ラズベリー（木苺）	razuberī
blackcurrant	クロスグリ	kuro suguri
redcurrant	フサスグリ	fusa suguri
gooseberry	セイヨウスグリ	seiyō suguri
cranberry	クランベリー	kuranberī
orange	オレンジ	orenji
mandarin	マンダリン	mandarin
pineapple	パイナップル	painappuru
banana	バナナ	banana
date	デーツ	dētsu
lemon	レモン	remon
apricot	アンズ [杏子]	anzu

peach	モモ［桃］	momo
kiwi	キウイ	kiui
grapefruit	グレープフルーツ	gurēbu furūtsu

berry	ベリー	berī
berries	ベリー	berī
cowberry	コケモモ	kokemomo
field strawberry	ノイチゴ［野いちご］	noichigo
bilberry	ビルベリー	biruberī

145. Flowers. Plants

| flower | 花 | hana |
| bouquet (of flowers) | 花束 | hanataba |

rose (flower)	バラ	bara
tulip	チューリップ	chūrippu
carnation	カーネーション	kānēshon
gladiolus	グラジオラス	gurajiorasu

cornflower	ヤグルマギク［矢車菊］	yagurumagiku
bluebell	ホタルブクロ	hotarubukuro
dandelion	タンポポ［蒲公英］	tanpopo
camomile	カモミール	kamomīru

aloe	アロエ	aroe
cactus	サボテン	saboten
rubber plant, ficus	イチジク	ichijiku

lily	ユリ［百合］	yuri
geranium	ゼラニウム	zeranyūmu
hyacinth	ヒヤシンス	hiyashinsu

mimosa	ミモザ	mimoza
narcissus	スイセン［水仙］	suisen
nasturtium	キンレンカ［金蓮花］	kinrenka

orchid	ラン［蘭］	ran
peony	シャクヤク［芍薬］	shakuyaku
violet	スミレ［菫］	sumire

pansy	パンジー	panjī
forget-me-not	ワスレナグサ［勿忘草］	wasurenagusa
daisy	デイジー	deijī

poppy	ポピー	popī
hemp	アサ［麻］	asa
mint	ミント	minto
lily of the valley	スズラン［鈴蘭］	suzuran
snowdrop	スノードロップ	sunōdoroppu

nettle	イラクサ [刺草]	irakusa
sorrel	スイバ	suiba
water lily	スイレン [睡蓮]	suiren
fern	シダ	shida
lichen	地衣類	chī rui

tropical greenhouse	温室	onshitsu
grass lawn	芝生	shibafu
flowerbed	花壇	kadan

plant	植物	shokubutsu
grass, herb	草	kusa
blade of grass	草の葉	kusa no ha

leaf	葉	ha
petal	花びら	hanabira
stem	茎	kuki
tuber	塊茎	kaikei

young plant (shoot)	シュート	shūto
thorn	茎針	kuki hari

to blossom (vi)	開花する	kaika suru
to fade, to wither	しおれる	shioreru
smell (odor)	香り	kaori
to cut (flowers)	切る	kiru
to pick (a flower)	摘む	tsumamu

146. Cereals, grains

grain	穀物	kokumotsu
cereal crops	禾穀類	kakokurui
ear (of barley, etc.)	花穂	kasui

wheat	コムギ [小麦]	komugi
rye	ライムギ [ライ麦]	raimugi
oats	オーツムギ [オーツ麦]	ōtsu mugi

millet	キビ [黍]	kibi
barley	オオムギ [大麦]	ōmugi

corn	トウモロコシ	tōmorokoshi
rice	イネ [稲]	ine
buckwheat	ソバ [蕎麦]	soba

pea plant	エンドウ [豌豆]	endō
kidney bean	インゲンマメ [隠元豆]	ingen mame
soy	ダイズ [大豆]	daizu
lentil	レンズマメ [レンズ豆]	renzu mame
beans (pulse crops)	豆類	mamerui

COUNTRIES. NATIONALITIES

147. Western Europe

Europe	ヨーロッパ	yōroppa
European Union	欧州連合	ōshū rengō
Austria	オーストリア	ōsutoria
Great Britain	グレートブリテン島	gurētoburiten tō
England	イギリス	igirisu
Belgium	ベルギー	berugī
Germany	ドイツ	doitsu
Netherlands	ネーデルラント	nēderuranto
Holland	オランダ	oranda
Greece	ギリシャ	girisha
Denmark	デンマーク	denmāku
Ireland	アイルランド	airurando
Iceland	アイスランド	aisurando
Spain	スペイン	supein
Italy	イタリア	itaria
Cyprus	キプロス	kipurosu
Malta	マルタ	maruta
Norway	ノルウェー	noruwē
Portugal	ポルトガル	porutogaru
Finland	フィンランド	finrando
France	フランス	furansu
Sweden	スウェーデン	suwēden
Switzerland	スイス	suisu
Scotland	スコットランド	sukottorando
Vatican	バチカン	bachikan
Liechtenstein	リヒテンシュタイン	rihitenshutain
Luxembourg	ルクセンブルク	rukusenburuku
Monaco	モナコ	monako

148. Central and Eastern Europe

Albania	アルバニア	arubania
Bulgaria	ブルガリア	burugaria
Hungary	ハンガリー	hangarī

Latvia	ラトピア	ratobia
Lithuania	リトアニア	ritoania
Poland	ポーランド	pōrando
Romania	ルーマニア	rūmania
Serbia	セルビア	serubia
Slovakia	スロバキア	surobakia
Croatia	クロアチア	kuroachia
Czech Republic	チェコ	cheko
Estonia	エストニア	esutonia
Bosnia-Herzegovina	ボスニア・ヘルツェゴヴィナ	bosunia herutsegovina
Macedonia	マケドニア地方	makedonia chihō
Slovenia	スロベニア	surobenia
Montenegro	モンテネグロ	monteneguro

149. Former USSR countries

Azerbaijan	アゼルバイジャン	azerubaijan
Armenia	アルメニア	arumenia
Belarus	ベラルーシー	berarūshī
Georgia	グルジア	gurujia
Kazakhstan	カザフスタン	kazafusutan
Kirghizia	キルギス	kirugisu
Moldavia	モルドヴァ	morudova
Russia	ロシア	roshia
Ukraine	ウクライナ	ukuraina
Tajikistan	タジキスタン	tajikisutan
Turkmenistan	トルクメニスタン	torukumenisutan
Uzbekistan	ウズベキスタン	uzubekisutan

150. Asia

Asia	アジア	ajia
Vietnam	ベトナム	betonamu
India	インド	indo
Israel	イスラエル	isuraeru
China	中国	chūgoku
Lebanon	レバノン	rebanon
Mongolia	モンゴル	mongoru
Malaysia	マレーシア	marēshia
Pakistan	パキスタン	pakisutan

Saudi Arabia	サウジアラビア	saujiarabia
Thailand	タイ	tai
Taiwan	台湾	taiwan
Turkey	トルコ	toruko
Japan	日本	nihon
Afghanistan	アフガニスタン	afuganisutan
Bangladesh	バングラデシュ	banguradeshu
Indonesia	インドネシア	indoneshia
Jordan	ヨルダン	yorudan
Iraq	イラク	iraku
Iran	イラン	iran
Cambodia	カンボジア	kanbojia
Kuwait	クウェート	kuwēto
Laos	ラオス	raosu
Myanmar	ミャンマー	myanmā
Nepal	ネパール	nepāru
United Arab Emirates	アラブ首長国連邦	arabu shuchō koku renpō
Syria	シリア	shiria
Palestine	パレスチナ	paresuchina
South Korea	大韓民国	daikanminkoku
North Korea	北朝鮮	kitachōsen

151. North America

United States of America	アメリカ合衆国	amerika gasshūkoku
Canada	カナダ	kanada
Mexico	メキシコ	mekishiko

152. Central and South America

Argentina	アルゼンチン	aruzenchin
Brazil	ブラジル	burajiru
Colombia	コロンビア	koronbia
Cuba	キューバ	kyūba
Chile	チリ	chiri
Bolivia	ボリビア	boribia
Venezuela	ベネズエラ	benezuera
Paraguay	パラグアイ	paraguai
Peru	ペルー	perū
Suriname	スリナム	surinamu
Uruguay	ウルグアイ	uruguai
Ecuador	エクアドル	ekuadoru

The Bahamas	パハマ	bahama
Haiti	ハイチ	haichi
Dominican Republic	ドミニカ共和国	dominikakyōwakoku
Panama	パナマ	panama
Jamaica	ジャマイカ	jamaika

153. Africa

Egypt	エジプト	ejiputo
Morocco	モロッコ	morokko
Tunisia	チュニジア	chunijia
Ghana	ガーナ	gāna
Zanzibar	ザンジバル	zanjibaru
Kenya	ケニア	kenia
Libya	リビア	ribia
Madagascar	マダガスカル	madagasukaru
Namibia	ナミビア	namibia
Senegal	セネガル	senegaru
Tanzania	タンザニア	tanzania
South Africa	南アフリカ	minami afurika

154. Australia. Oceania

Australia	オーストラリア	ōsutoraria
New Zealand	ニュージーランド	nyūjīrando
Tasmania	タスマニア	tasumania
French Polynesia	フランス領ポリネシア	furansu ryō porineshia

155. Cities

Amsterdam	アムステルダム	amusuterudamu
Ankara	アンカラ	ankara
Athens	アテネ	atene
Baghdad	バグダッド	bagudaddo
Bangkok	バンコク	bankoku
Barcelona	バルセロナ	baruserona
Beijing	北京	pekin
Beirut	ベイルート	beirūto
Berlin	ベルリン	berurin
Bombay, Mumbai	ムンバイ	munbai
Bonn	ボン	bon

Bordeaux	ボルドー	borudō
Bratislava	ブラチスラヴァ	burachisurava
Brussels	ブリュッセル	buryusseru
Bucharest	ブカレスト	bukaresuto
Budapest	ブダペスト	budapesuto
Cairo	カイロ	kairo
Calcutta	コルカタ	korukata
Chicago	シカゴ	shikago
Copenhagen	コペンハーゲン	kopenhāgen
Dar-es-Salaam	ダルエスサラーム	daruesusarāmu
Delhi	デリー	derī
Dubai	ドバイ	dobai
Dublin	ダブリン	daburin
Düsseldorf	デュッセルドルフ	dyusserudorufu
Florence	フィレンチェ	firenche
Frankfurt	フランクフルト	furankufuruto
Geneva	ジュネーブ	junēbu
The Hague	ハーグ	hāgu
Hamburg	ハンブルク	hanburuku
Hanoi	ハノイ	hanoi
Havana	ハバナ	habana
Helsinki	ヘルシンキ	herushinki
Hiroshima	広島	hiroshima
Hong Kong	香港	honkon
Istanbul	イスタンブール	isutanbūru
Jerusalem	エルサレム	erusaremu
Kiev	キエフ	kiefu
Kuala Lumpur	クアラルンプール	kuararunpūru
Lisbon	リスボン	risubon
London	ロンドン	rondon
Los Angeles	ロスアンジェルス	rosuanjerusu
Lyons	リヨン	riyon
Madrid	マドリード	madorīdo
Marseille	マルセイユ	maruseiyu
Mexico City	メキシコシティ	mekishiko shiti
Miami	マイアミ	maiami
Montreal	モントリオール	montoriōru
Moscow	モスクワ	mosukuwa
Munich	ミュンヘン	myunhen
Nairobi	ナイロビ	nairobi
Naples	ナポリ	napori
New York	ニューヨーク	nyūyōku
Nice	ニース	nīsu
Oslo	オスロ	osuro
Ottawa	オタワ	otawa

Paris	パリ	pari
Prague	プラハ	puraha
Rio de Janeiro	リオ・デ・ジャネイロ	rio de janeiro
Rome	ローマ	rōma

Saint Petersburg	サンクトペテルブルク	sankuto peteruburuku
Seoul	ソウル	sōru
Shanghai	上海	shanhai
Singapore	シンガポール	shingapōru
Stockholm	ストックホルム	sutokkuhorumu
Sydney	シドニー	shidonī

Taipei	台北	taipei
Tokyo	東京	tōkyō
Toronto	トロント	toronto

Venice	ベニス	benisu
Vienna	ウィーン	wīn
Warsaw	ワルシャワ	warushawa
Washington	ワシントン	washinton

CPSIA information can be obtained
at www.ICGtesting.com
Printed in the USA
LVOW04s2312260716
497924LV00027B/601/P